D0869870

Mickey
MANTLE
Memories and Memorabilia

Edited by Larry Canale

Copyright ©2011 F+W Media, Inc.

All rights reserved. No portion of this publication may be reproduced or transmitted in any form or by any means, electronic or mechanical, including photocopy, recording, or any information storage and retrieval system, without permission in writing from the publisher, except by a reviewer who may quote brief passages in a critical article or review to be printed in a magazine or newspaper, or electronically transmitted on radio, television, or the Internet.

Published by

Krause Publications, a division of F+W Media, Inc.
700 East State Street • Iola, WI 54990-0001
715-445-2214 • 888-457-2873
www.krausebooks.com

To order books or other products call toll-free 1-800-258-0929
or visit us online at www.krausebooks.com or www.Shop.Collect.com

ISBN-13: 978-1-4402-1543-8
ISBN-10: 1-4402-1543-X

Cover Design by Rachael Wolter
Designed by Shawn Williams

Printed in China

DEDICATION

For my family, especially my softball-slugging daughters Quinlyn and Karsyn and for my parents, the ultimate Yankees fans.

ACKNOWLEDGEMENTS

The archives of Sports Collectors Digest and Tuff Stuff's Sports Collectors Monthly were key sources of text, background material, research, and artwork in the editing and compilation of Mickey Mantle: Memories & Memorabilia. So kudos, thanks, and appreciation to all of the writers and editors whose work is represented and reflected in these pages, especially T.S. O'Connell, Rick Hines, Mark Larson, Dave Platta, and Kelly Eisenhauer.

Photographs were provided by Getty Images, Heritage Auction Galleries, Robert Edward Auctions, and Guernsey's. Thank you.

Special thanks to baseball expert, publicist, and writer Marty Appel and to author and noted Mantle collector Randall Swearingen. I'd also like to thank Leila Dunbar, Mike Gutierrez, and Simeon Lipman, Mantle memorabilia experts who shared their information and perspective.

Very special acknowledgement to author and editor Daniel Sullivan for his Mantle recollections, feedback, and advice; to Toni Monkovic, the sports copy desk chief at The New York Times; and to Ozzie Sweet, whose portraits of Mickey Mantle throughout his career have provided a wonderful photographic record of "The Magnificent Yankee."

Finally, I would like to extend my sincere appreciation to all of those baseball fans who took the time to share their memories of Mickey Mantle for this project. Your anecdotes and observations of No. 7 collectively offer a unique perspective and a worthy window into a golden era of baseball and the game's most dynamic star.

CONTENTS

A Picture-Perfect Memory of Mantle

By Ozzie Sweet

FACING:

By the early 1960s, Mantle was a hero to millions of American boys, a fact not lost on photographer Ozzie Sweet.

©Ozzie Sweet

RIGHT:

A baby-faced Mantle photographed by Sweet in spring training in 1952.

©Ozzie Sweet

IT WAS 58 YEARS AND THOUSANDS of photographic subjects ago, but I do remember meeting Mickey Mantle for the first time. How could I forget? It was a warm spring day in St. Petersburg, Florida, in 1952, which was to be Mickey's first full season in the big leagues. For me, it marked the first of what would be dozens of portrait sessions with baseball's most herculean star. The New York Yankees' training camp that year was bursting with energy and confidence and a certain hopefulness, all of which you would expect from baseball's world champions.

With Joe DiMaggio having just retired, the biggest buzz in 1952 centered on young Mickey. He was only 20 but had already played in a World Series, had already suffered a serious knee injury that cut short his World Series, had already been tabbed as the replacement for Joe DiMaggio.

At the time, I was five years into a career as a freelance cover photographer, having left a position as *Newsweek*'s chief cover photographer in 1948. I had worked hard to place my "photographic illustrations" on a wide variety of publications but the images that attracted the most attention were the ones I was creating for *Sport* magazine.

When I left my home base in Connecticut to travel to Florida in February 1952, I had instructions from *Sport* editor Ed Fitzgerald to get a selection of portraits of Mickey. Ed wanted the kinds of close-up studies I had done with DiMaggio, Bob Feller, Ted Williams, Jackie Robinson, and others. I set out to make it happen, working with the Yankees' PR men to line up a session with Mantle. As always, I studied up on my subject. Mickey was billed as the next Babe Ruth, Lou Gehrig, and DiMaggio all rolled into one. Not only was he mighty with the bat, but he could run like the wind. Manager Casey Stengel had seen a lot of players in his years, but never one like Mickey. He told the press in 1951, "That kid can hit balls over buildings."

With some players, that kind of hype might go to their heads. But when Mickey showed up for our first portrait session, I could tell instantly that he was a shy and quiet kid. The thing I remember most was how very young he looked—he was baby-faced and still had a little bit of a complexion problem. He was also very serious; during that first session, there was hardly a hint of the smile that would come so easy in our future sessions.

A photographer tends to look closely at his subject's face, and what I saw was a country kid who felt the pressure of replacing a legend on America's favorite team. Yet I could also see a real determination in Mickey's eyes; I see it even now when I look at those first portraits we did together.

I say "together" because it was very much a collaborative effort. Within just a couple of years, Mickey went from painfully shy to fully confident. By the time of his 1956 Triple Crown season, he was a picture of confidence. Gone were the complexion issues and the shyness; in their place: a smooth-skinned face and a bright smile. And those eyes …. Mickey almost always had a smile in his eyes. A photographer doesn't always achieve that in a subject, but with Mickey it was part of a look that made him my favorite subject.

By the early 1960s, I was trying to create photographs that showed Mickey the way fans saw him, or the way they wished they could see him—standing at home plate with a bat in his hands as he stared at the pitcher, or in a follow-through pose as he looked

Mantle shared the Yankee Stadium spotlight with Roger Maris in 1961 during one of the greatest home run races in baseball history. *©Ozzie Sweet*

off in the distance after hitting another homer. Mickey had such a muscular build that when he struck a batting pose, he looked imposing. One of his personal favorites, he later told me, came from that era—a photograph I took from behind as he leaned on a bat. That big No. 7 on his back and his recognizable profile jumped off the photograph. I've always said that Mickey not only hit the ball farther than anyone, he could even lean on his bat better than anyone.

By the early 1960s, Mickey went above and beyond the concept of "cooperative." One year, he saw me arrive in camp and gave me a wonderful greeting: "Hey Ozz, what kind of crazy things have you got in store for us this year?" It always made me feel good to get that kind of willingness. Ballplayers, after all, get tugged in a million directions by the press, family, friends, and teammates, and Mickey got tugged more than anyone. But it didn't stop him from being cooperative.

FACING:
Early in the 1957 season, *Sport* magazine sent Sweet to Yankee Stadium to photograph Mantle with Billy Martin and Whitey Ford, his "partners in crime." *©Ozzie Sweet*

As the years rolled on, I witnessed through my camera's viewfinder the maturing of this great baseball hero, and every session seemed to get better, right up until 1969, when a freshly retired Mickey and his son Mickey Jr. posed on the beaches of Ft. Lauderdale, not far from the Yankees' camp at the time, for a colorful fashion spread for *Boys' Life* magazine.

Yet of all the color portraits I took of Mickey between 1952 and 1969, the most memorable photographs were actually black-and-white grabs that didn't have a baseball, bat, glove, or pinstripes in sight. In early April 1957, spring training had wound down and the players were getting ready to head north. Before the Yankees' departure, I got the idea to invite Mickey on a fishing trip. He took me up on the offer, so I asked him who else we should bring along. He responded with the names of three of his best Yankees pals—Whitey Ford, Billy Martin, and Bob Grim. We met at the docks on the west coast of Florida at 5:30 one morning and off we sailed, with a cooler full of sodas and basket of fried chicken in tow. I had my camera loaded with black and white film, and so all morning, as my Yankee friends enjoyed themselves, I took candid shots of them relaxing and laughing and telling stories and catching fish and generally having a hell of a good time. Just looking at those images again brings me back onto that boat, where I can hear the laughter of young Mickey at one of the happiest times in his life, fresh off a Triple Crown season and poised to go out and conquer the world in 1957.

I've been very fortunate during my career to have captured thousands of faces on film. I remember so many of them, too. There have been beautiful female models (including my wife Diane) and handsome male ones. There have been average but attractive folks who did wonderful jobs of posing. There have been all kinds of innocent-faced children (including my own), not to mention any number of pets and even wild animals. I've enjoyed capturing the faces of all kinds of celebrities: Albert Einstein and Dwight Eisenhower, Bob Hope and Helen Hayes, Jimmy Durante and Arthur Godfrey, Ingrid Bergman and (before she became Princess of Monaco) Grace Kelly.

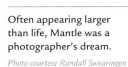

Often appearing larger than life, Mantle was a photographer's dream.

Photo courtesy Randall Swearingen

But I probably had more fun photographing athletes than anyone else, whether it was a chiseled football hero like Jim Brown or John Unitas, a muscular prize-fighter like Rocky Marciano or Joe Louis, a hockey Hall of Famer like Maurice Richard or Bobby Orr, or a basketball legend like George Mikan or Oscar Robertson, or a golfing great like Jack Nicklaus. And there were all those baseball stars: DiMaggio and Williams and Willie Mays and Hank Aaron and Roberto Clemente. But the one who has stayed foremost in my memory is Mickey Mantle. He was a photographer's dream, and he was a friend I'll never forget.

FACING:

After finishing spring training in 1956, Sweet took Mantle, Bob Grim, Billy Martin and Whitey Ford on a fishing excursion off Madeira Beach on the Gulf of Mexico. This relaxed shot, capturing the camaraderie of the outing, became a popular photograph among collectors.

*In a career that began in the early 1940s, **Ozzie Sweet** has accounted for more than 1,750 magazine covers. He's best known for his portraits of athletes on* Sport *magazine from 1948 through the mid-1960s and for his* Newsweek *covers in the 1940s. But his work has also appeared on* Time, Sports Illustrated, Saturday Evening Post, Cosmopolitan, Family Circle, *and legions of other publications. His photography also has filled dozens of books, including 18 wildlife titles in the 1970s and 1980s plus* Legends of the Field *(1993),* Mickey Mantle: The Yankees Years *(1998), and* The Boys of Spring *(2005). He's also working on a new book called* America's Cover Photographer.

A Fragile, Magnificent Hero

By Larry Canale

I REMEMBER THE DAY MICKEY MANTLE DIED: Aug. 13, 1995. It was a Sunday morning, I know, because I got a wake-up call from a reporter who asked, "Can you give me a quote about Mantle?" At the time, I was working as editor of the sports memorabilia magazine *Tuff Stuff,* so the reporter's request wasn't a bizarre one — except that it came at daybreak on Sunday. So even in a groggy state, I was able to ask a logical question: "Why do you need a Mantle quote on a Sunday morning?"

His response: "You didn't hear? Mickey died last night."

The news was stunning to me, even though Mantle's ambulance trip to a hospital in May 1995 and his battle with liver cancer and his organ transplant and his bleak prognosis had been well publicized for weeks. It was Mickey Mantle. He *can't* die.

Just a year and two months earlier, in June 1994, I met Mantle in a Richmond, Virginia, hotel room for an interview. I waited for him outside his suite's master bedroom when he suddenly emerged: *Mickey Mantle,* in person. The sight of him was, in a way, stunning (there's that word again). He was hale and hearty and had a robust handshake and quick smile. He looked every bit the hero that I had read about and studied and idolized as a kid.

FACING:

Few baseball players have captured the sports world's imagination like the great Mickey Mantle.

Kidwiler Collection/Getty Images

RIGHT:

A 1952 Topps Mickey Mantle card has a book value of $250,000 but can sell for more than $300,000 if it's in Gem Mint condition.

And for the next 45 minutes, he was an interviewer's dream. He spun stories about his early days and about Casey and Yogi and Whitey. He reflected on his favorite accomplishments, like his Triple Crown season in 1956 (.353, 52 homers, and 130 RBI —with 132 runs and 10 stolen bases to boot) and on his regrets (like the fact that his career batting average dropped below .300 in his final season, when he hit .237).

He talked about how moving it was to meet awestruck, trembling fans at autograph shows around the nation. "I have guys come through," he told me, "and they get tears in their eyes, and they say, 'Mickey, I've waited 30 years to meet you! … And they'll have their kids with them and they'll say, 'Son, this is Mickey Mantle, the greatest player.' Hell, I get goose-bumps sometimes just talking to these guys."

I knew just how "these guys" felt—even though I was born too late to see vintage Mantle in action. It was 1968 when I started caring about baseball, so I actually thought of him as a first baseman. One of my earliest memories as a suddenly baseball-obsessed kid was reading the sad line—with an exclamation mark, strangely — on the back of The Mick's 1969 Topps baseball card: "The All-Star announced his retirement from baseball on March 1st, 1969!"

Around the same time, I read and re-read (and re-read again) a *Sport* feature tagged with the line "Farewell to Mickey Mantle." The cover photo was an Ozzie Sweet portrait of a heroic-looking Mickey, Yankees cap in hand, gazing off into the sunset. That year, 1969, Bobby Murcer became my "active" idol, but Mantle was my all-time hero, so I did what any kid would do. I backtracked through his career, memorizing the stats and records and World Series heroics. I watched clips of his drag bunts and his "web gems" covering Yankee Stadium's vast center field, and I read about his switch-hitting tendencies (he batted .281 with 369 homers in 5,253 at-bats as a lefty, and .329 with 160 homers in 2,728 at-bats from the right side). I pored over countless stories about the injuries that shortened his career, wondering (like all fans did): "What if...?"

Most of all, I envied all of those Yankee fans who watched No. 7 play in his prime. He must have been a sight to see.

This extraordinary signed Old Timers' Day photo from 1984 features the signatures of three of the greatest players in New York Yankees history: Joe DiMaggio, Mickey Mantle, and Roger Maris. Maris did not attend many Yankees Old Timers' Day ceremonies and it is believed this photo was taken when the Yankees retired Maris' number 9. This historical piece sold for $1,880 at a Robert Edward Auctions.

After four decades of alcohol abuse, Mantle described his life of self-destructive behavior and hopes for recovery in a straightforward and emotional cover story in *Sports Illustrated*, April 18, 1994.

Heritage Auctions Galleries

The New York Yankees team members line up to pay their final respects to baseball great Mickey Mantle during a two-minute moment of silence before a home game with Cleveland on August 13, 1995. Mantle died of cancer in Dallas earlier in the day.

JON LEVY/AFP/Getty Images

ABOVE:
Eleven members of the 500 Home Run Club signed this Ron Lewis print. From left to right: Ted Williams, Frank Robinson, Harmon Killebrew, Reggie Jackson, Mickey Mantle, Willie Mays, Hank Aaron, Mike Schmidt, Ernie Banks, Eddie Mathews, and Willie McCovey. The artist also signed this piece, which sold at a Robert Edward Auctions for $1,400.

FACING:
This 1962 Mickey Mantle original painting by famed sports artist LeRoy Neiman sold for $119,500 in November 2010 at Heritage Auction Galleries.

THE ULTIMATE MICKEY MANTLE

World Series home run ticket display

THE ULTIMATE MICKEY MANTLE WORLD SERIES DISPLAY
Mickey Mantle's total of 18 home runs in World Series play ranks as one of the most impressive records in baseball history. This spectacular wall display (40 x 52.5 inches) features not only ticket stubs from each of the 16 World Series games in which Mantle hit a home run, but individual cut signatures of the 15 pitchers victimized by Mantle. In the center of the display is a large 16 x 20-inch signed black-and-white photo of Mantle. A special plaque below the photo makes note of Mantle's World Series home run record, while individual plaques below each ticket list the pertinent details from that game (date, score, pitcher of record, inning of home run).

The display's 15 cut signatures, scripted in various inks, are those of Billy Loes, Joe Black, Preacher Roe, Russ Meyer, Johnny Podres, Sal Maglie, Ed Roebuck, Gene Conley, Lew Burdette, Freddie Green, Joe Gibbon, Sandy Koufax, Barney Schultz, Curt Simmons, and Bob Gibson. Mantle signed the large central photo in blue Sharpie. The one minor flaw is the fact that the 1963 Game 4 ticket and the 1964 Game 3 ticket were mistakenly transposed during the framing process, and each is mounted above the wrong descriptive plaque. The individual pieces comprising the display, of course, have a very substantial "break value" but the true value of this piece is as an extraordinary museum-caliber Mickey Mantle World Series display. It sold at Robert Edward Auctions for $6,463.

The tickets comprising the display are:

- 1952: Game 6 at Brooklyn
- 1952: Game 7 at Brooklyn
- 1953: Game 2 at New York
- 1953: Game 5 at Brooklyn
- 1955: Game 3 at Brooklyn
- 1956: Game 1 at Brooklyn
- 1956: Game 4 at New York
- 1956: Game 5 at New York
  (Don Larsen's perfect game)
- 1957: Game 3 at Milwaukee
- 1958: Game 2 at Milwaukee
  (two home runs, both off of Lew Burdette)
- 1960: Game 2 at Pittsburgh
  (two home runs, one off of Freddie Green, the other off of Joe Gibbon)
- 1960: Game 3 at New York
- 1963: Game 4 at Los Angeles
- 1964: Game 3 at New York
- 1964: Game 6 at St. Louis
- 1964: Game 7 at St. Louis

Showcasing some of the greatest players of their era, this selection of signed Perez-Steele Hall of Fame postcards features (clockwise from upper left) Ted Williams, Joe DiMaggio, Mickey Mantle, Willie Mays, Eddie Mathews, and Hank Aaron.

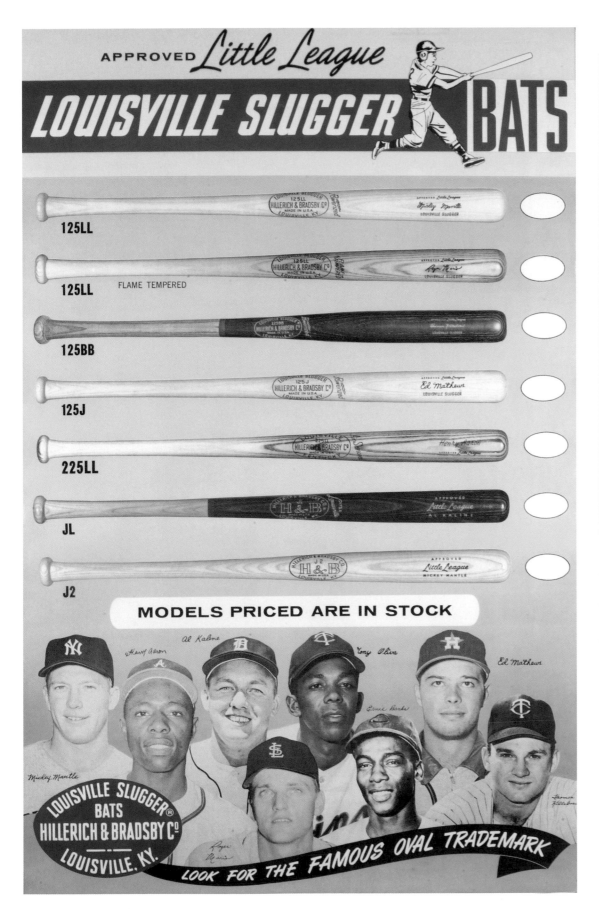

This exceedingly rare retail poster (22.5 x 35.5 inches), which showcases the Hillerich & Bradsby line of Little League bats for the 1967 season, features endorsements from eight of the game's top stars: Mickey Mantle, Roger Maris, Hank Aaron, Al Kaline, Eddie Mathews, Ernie Banks, Tony Oliva, and Harmon Killebrew. All eight players are pictured along the bottom, while examples of the various Louisville Slugger Little League bats for sale are pictured above. This poster was issued only to participating retailers and was intended for display on store walls in promotion of the company's most recent line of Little League bats. As clearly noted along the top, all of the Louisville Sluggers pictured here are "Approved Little League Bats." Given the star power of its endorsers, it's no surprise that Louisville Slugger bats were the bat of choice for nearly every youngster in America at the time. The poster was never displayed in a store (all of the spaces reserved for the retailer to write in prices are blank) and is an exceptional display piece from an era that has very few store-display pieces of this type or caliber. It sold at Robert Edward Auctions for $7,050.

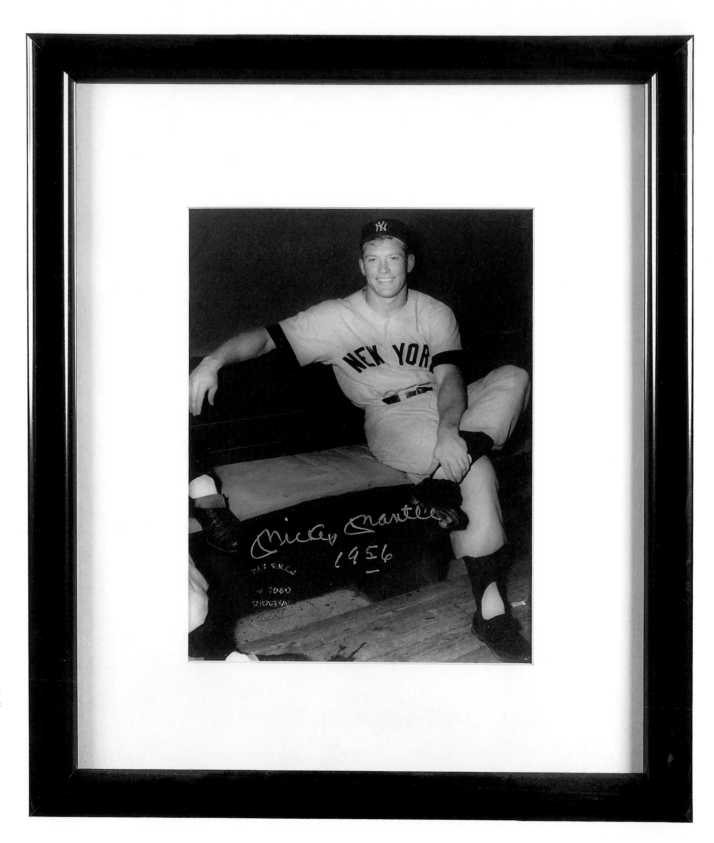

This popular Ray Gallo dugout portrait of Mantle bears his oh-so-desired signature with Mantle's favorite "1956" inscription, referencing his Triple Crown season.

Heritage Auction Galleries

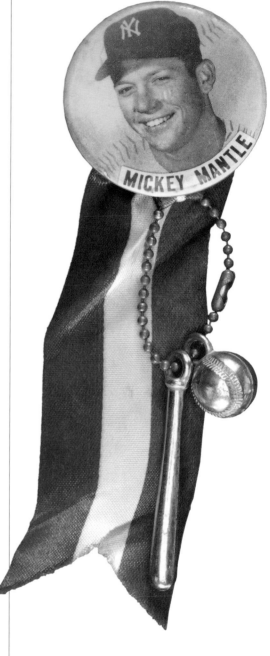

This Artist's Proof signed photograph is a very limited edition from Upper Deck Authenticated. The masterful and large (11x17-inch) color portrait is numbered one of a run of ten and signed by Mantle.

Almost as famous for his carousing and boozing as he was for his tape measure home run blasts, Mantle surely wasn't at his best when he laid Sharpie to photograph for a fan. After a successful "Best wishes" greeting, Mantle falters with the formation of the first letter of his given name. He then goes on to complete his autograph and add the explanation "With the Shakes." And so this rather ugly autograph becomes desirable to collectors, as it speaks to both the demons that haunted this magnetic star throughout his life, and the terrific sense of humor for which he was also beloved. This photo sold at Heritage Auction Galleries for $956.

Heritage Auction Galleries

Mantle hit 536 career home runs, ranking 16th on Major League Baseball's all-time list. In 1999, *The Sporting News* placed Mantle at 17th on its list of "The 100 Greatest Baseball Players."

Heritage Auction Galleries

chapter one

Humble Beginnings

BELOW:
Even with eyes closed, you could see young Mick Mantle was something special.

FACING:
Two years before Mantle joined the New York Yankees he wore the pinstripes of the 1949 Independence (Kansas) Yankees of the Kansas-Oklahoma-Missouri League. That's the future legend kneeling at far right and, comically, the only player to blink when the photographer snapped the shutter. The photo comes from the personal collection of Bob Wiesler (top row, fourth from right), who was a rookie with Mantle on the 1951 New York Yankees.

Heritage Auction Galleries

THERE'S NOTHING TOUGHER IN SPORTS THAN LIVING UP TO HYPE. Once you're labeled "the next this" or "the second coming of that," you're living under a microscope while trying to live up to inflated expectations and dealing with the pressure that comes with them.

In the case of Mickey Charles Mantle, the label happened to be his first name. His baseball-crazy father, Elvin "Mutt" Mantle, admired Mickey Cochrane of the Philadelphia Athletics, a catcher who hit .331 in 1929, .357 in 1930, and .349 in 1931. So when Mutt's first son entered the world on October 20, 1931, he received the name Mickey.

The Mantles lived in Spavinaw, Oklahoma, in the far northeast corner of the state. Life was tough in those parts in the 1930s, when the Great Depression was reaching its depths. Oklahoma was the great Dust Bowl—a region suffering from a great drought that drove thousands of people from their farms. They headed west to California hoping for a land of milk and honey but willing to settle for a job and just enough money to get by.

Mutt Mantle, though, stayed in Oklahoma, although he did move his family from Spavinaw to nearby Commerce. Mickey was 4 years old at the time. Mutt worked

JOE MOUNTFORD
PRESIDENT

MARY ANN HOWARD
VICE-PRES.

CAROLE SHAMBLIN
SECRETARY

Juniors

| DONNIE DODD | NEVA LE SPEAKER | BILL MOSLEY | JUNE PHARIS | MICKEY MANTLE |

| RUBY SHELTON | J. D. SHOUSE | RODNEY GAMBLE | DOROTHY ANN CRESAP | JO ANN WALKER |

| GLENN HENSLEY | LEROY TRASK | KATHLEEN BEARD | SHIRLEY JUDD | JOE JOHNSON |

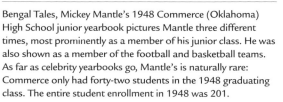

Bengal Tales, Mickey Mantle's 1948 Commerce (Oklahoma) High School junior yearbook pictures Mantle three different times, most prominently as a member of his junior class. He was also shown as a member of the football and basketball teams. As far as celebrity yearbooks go, Mantle's is naturally rare: Commerce only had forty-two students in the 1948 graduating class. The entire student enrollment in 1948 was 201.

Robert Edward Auctions

for Eagle-Picher Zinc & Lead Co., one of many mining companies operating in northeastern Oklahoma, southwestern Missouri, and southeastern Kansas. He did everything from shoveling ore to breaking boulders to working as a muleskinner until he was promoted to ground supervisor.

And on weekends, he played baseball. Boy, did he play baseball.

Mutt Mantle, a switch-hitter who could run and had a good arm, loved the game and played in local leagues, as his father did. Although Mutt never had a chance to advance beyond the town team, his baseball influence on young Mickey was immense. Among the skills he pushed on him: switch-hitting, from the first time he picked up a bat. As Mickey was growing up, he batted lefty against his father (who threw right-handed) and right-handed against his grandfather, Charlie Mantle (a lefty). The men would alternate turns pitching to Mickey, who soon became comfortable hitting from both sides of the plate.

Times were tough in Commerce, and Mutt's work was taxing. Not only was the pay low, but the mine's dust caused serious illness among the miners and their families. By the time Mickey was 13, his grandfather and two of his uncles were dead of Hodgkin's disease, a form of cancer of the lymph nodes. It's unknown as to whether the disease was hereditary in the Mantle family or a result of working in the mines, but it scarred Mickey's outlook on life, especially when the disease claimed his father a decade later.

Certainly, Mutt Mantle recognized the hazards and problems of being a miner, so he moved his family—which now included five children—away from Commerce. He traded the deed to his house for a tractor, a horse, some cattle, and the right to work as a sharecropper on a farm owned by a local doctor.

The farm provided room for the Mantle kids—twins Roy and Ray, Barbara, and Larry, nicknamed Butch—to run. Despite all the hard work that Mutt, wife Lovell, and the five Mantle kids did, farm life didn't last long. Mutt's dreams were destroyed by the same problem that drove Okies off their land during the Dust Bowl days: the weather. It wasn't a lack of rain that did them in; ironically, a fall flood cost the Mantles their farm.

After several days of rain just before harvest time, the Neosho River overflowed its banks, filling the creek on the Mantles' farm. Crops were ruined and the family was driven from its home, forced to move to a two-room shack just outside Commerce that didn't

have indoor plumbing. Getting two adults, five children, and all their possessions into two rooms took some ingenuity.

When you're living in poverty, there has to be an escape. For Mickey, that escape was sports. He was big, quick, strong, and fast—an athlete who could set the heart of any football, baseball, or basketball coach racing. During his sophomore year at Commerce High School, Mantle was convinced by a friend to go out for the football team, despite his father's objections that he'd get hurt and ruin his budding baseball career. Events later showed that Mutt Mantle knew what he was talking about; Mickey, a running back, didn't make it through his first season on the gridiron.

Things were going well until Mickey sustained an injury during a practice, nearly bringing his fledgling athletic career to an untimely end. Mickey was carrying the ball when a tackler kicked him in the left shin. At the time, the injury didn't look very serious, so the coach, who thought it was a sprain, told Mickey to go home and soak his leg. It wasn't a sprain, however. More likely, it was a deep bone bruise with internal bleeding.

The day after the injury, Mickey woke up with a raging fever. His left ankle was swollen to twice its normal size. When doctors at the nearby Picher hospital examined the leg, they concluded the wound was superficial but they were worried about Mickey's high fever. They lanced the ankle and treated it with compresses and liniments, hoping to slow the swelling. Nothing seemed to work.

Finally, osteomyelitis set in. Osteomyelitis is a bacterial infection of bone that can deteriorate it enough to kill the bone tissue. At the time, osteomyelitis was considered a deadly disease, claiming many lives. To save Mickey's life, doctors in Oklahoma in 1946 considered amputating the leg.

Mickey's parents objected strenuously. Lovell Mantle, not about to let her son lose his leg, went to a lawyer in nearby Miami, Oklahoma, who drew up papers transferring Mickey to the state hospital for children in Oklahoma City. There, doctors used a new drug to control the inflammation in Mickey's leg. Six daily penicillin injections into the injured limb led to dramatic improvement. Mickey left the hospital soon after but was so weak (he had lost some 45 pounds, dropping to around 110) he had to be carried out by one of his brothers.

A long stretch of rehabilitation was ahead for Mantle, mainly because the osteomyelitis could flare up again (as it would later, throughout his baseball career). However, the resilient 15-year-old

To understand just how beloved the New York Yankees were, consider that teammates Babe Ruth and Lou Gehrig toured the countryside in 1927 and 1928 playing postseason exhibition games to capitalize on their unbridled popularity. This original photo of Ruth and Gehrig was issued as a souvenir during their famous 1928 "Bustin' Babes and Larrupin' Lou's" barnstorming tour, signed by each in blue fountain pen. The 8 x 10-inch photo captures the two stars posing together in their respective tour uniforms and features the facsimile signatures of both Ruth and Gehrig, as issued. The actual signatures of Ruth and Gehrig appear directly below their respective facsimile examples. The Bustin' Babes and Larrupin' Lou's barnstorming tour was the brainchild of Christy Walsh, who was Ruth and Gehrig's longtime agent. The tour, heralded as "Ruth vs. Gehrig - The Battle For The Home Run Title Continues," began in New York and made its away across the country, ending in California. Walsh arranged it so Ruth and Gehrig were the only two players traveling to each town. Their respective teams at each venue were made up of local players. The tour was a huge success, with most games ending prematurely due to fans rushing onto the field to get closer to their idols. In addition to the gate revenues, one of the other main sources of income during the tour came from the sale of these special tour photos for $1, a large sum at the time. One of the finest examples of these highly prized photos, this item brought $17,625 at Robert Edward Auctions.

BABE RUTH
AND
LOU GEHRIG

BASEBALL'S GREATEST ATTRACTIONS

Reserved Seats on Sale at Neil House Cigar Stand

See the Emperor of Swat and the Crown Prince in Nine Innings of Baseball

DAYTON
Thursday, October 25th

Boys under 16 years, 50c

Game Starts at 3:00 P.M.

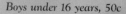

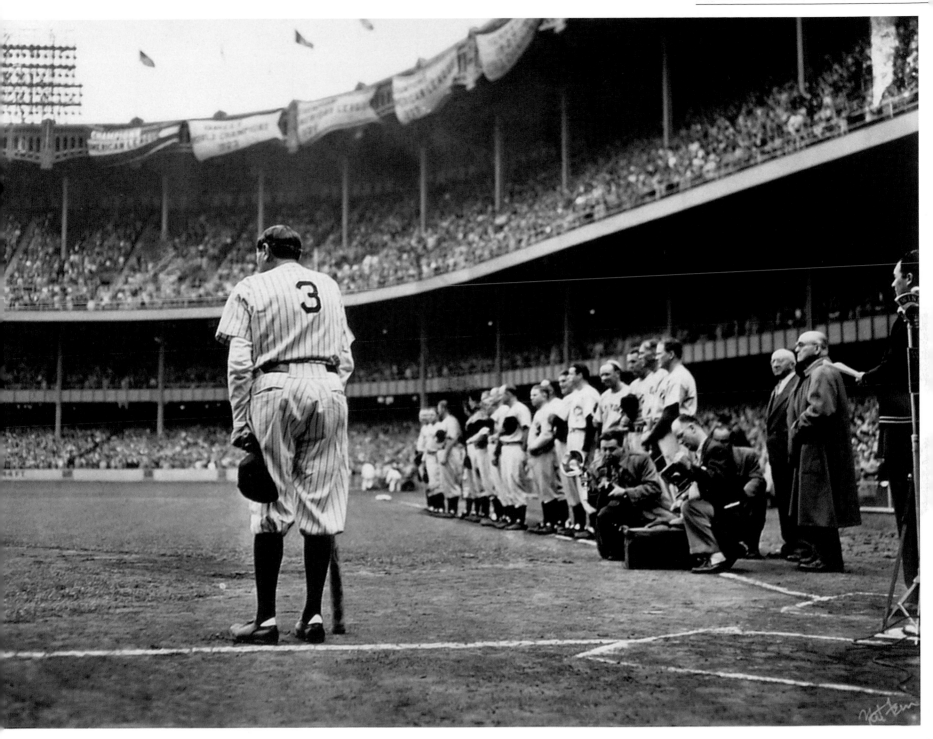

As Mantle's baseball career was starting, a bigger-than-life story was coming to an end. This large-format (16 x 20-inch) photo, "The Babe Bows Out," earned photographer Nat Fein (1914-2000) the Pulitzer Prize for photography and is featured in both the Baseball Hall of Fame and the Smithsonian Institute. The haunting image captures Babe Ruth during his final appearance at Yankee Stadium in 1948.

The image remains the most enduring image of Ruth ever taken and is one of the most famous sports photographs of all time. The photo was taken June 13, 1948, when the Yankees commemorated the 25th anniversary of Yankee Stadium by inviting all the members of the 1923 team to join them in the celebration. In conjunction with that ceremony, the team also chose to honor Ruth by retiring his number. Ruth was gravely ill with cancer at the time; he died just two months later. Fein, a photographer for the New York Herald Tribune, knelt behind Ruth, aimed his Speed Graphic camera, and captured a priceless moment in American sports history. Fein was asked why he took the shot without showing Ruth's face. "The retiring of No. 3 was the story," Fein explained. "You didn't need to see the Babe's face to recognize him. You'd recognize his great hulk and spindly legs anyplace. No one else had that particular angle, so it was a little something different." The photograph sold for $9,400 in a Robert Edward Auctions.

It was easy to see why Mutt Mantle so wanted his son to play for the New York Yankees. The team was filled with great players and it won. The team would win an unprecedented four straight World Series titles from 1936 to 1939. In only his second year with the New York Yankees, Joe DiMaggio had emerged as a star player and one of the most popular players in the league. This original Associated Press wirephoto, culled from *The Detroit News* archives, captures DiMaggio signing autographs for fans during the 1937 World Series at the Polo Grounds. The Yankees would defeat the Giants in five games for the title, the second in as many years for DiMaggio.

Robert Edward Auctions

In the years to come, Mantle would replace the great Joe DiMaggio in the New York Yankees outfield. But in 1939 there was a changing of the guard of another sort for the Yankees. Culled from The Chicago Sun Times archives this photograph captures Lou Gehrig and DiMaggio during their final season together. The caption on the back of the photo provides a haunting foreshadowing of things to come: "A camera study of the two great men of the New York Yankees; (left) young Joe DiMaggio, who though he is already the best outfielder in his league, seems certain to rival Ty Cobb within the next few seasons for the honor of being the No. 1 outfielder of all time; (right) old Lou Gehrig, fading "iron man" of the national game and once fabulous hitter who is now paying his second visit to Comiskey Park as a noncombatant, one who sits on the bench of afternoons and considers a trip to the Mayo Clinic instead of to the plate." No one really understood what was wrong with Gehrig in 1939, but they would in less than two weeks time. Gehrig entered the Mayo Clinic on May 13th, just five days after this photo was taken. At the end of his week-long examination, doctors diagnosed his condition as amyotrophic lateral sclerosis, a terminal disease of the central nervous system for which there was, and still is, no cure. Gehrig died June 2, 1939.

Robert Edward Auctions

chapter two

1950-1955: The Early Years

AS AUGUST TURNED TO SEPTEMBER IN THE SUMMER OF 1950, the Yankees were locked in a tight pennant race with two other American League teams. The Detroit Tigers and Boston Red Sox were bunched up within three games of the Yankees. The race only got tighter when New York lost three of its first six games in September.

By Sept. 17, the three contenders were even tighter:
1) New York Yankees   89-51-1
2) Detroit Tigers   88-51-3
3) Boston Red Sox   87-53-0

What better time to expose your most promising prospect to the big leagues than a pressure-filled pennant race? That was the Yankees' thinking when they called up 18-year-old switch-hitting shortstop Mickey Mantle, fresh off a .383, 26-homer season with the Joplin (Mo.) Miners.

Actually, it wasn't a typical call-up. Despite hitting .383 with 26 home runs for the Joplin (Missouri) Miners, the Yankees were looking for help from their switch-hitting shortstop. In fact, the Yankee brass didn't even activate Mantle; rather, he was invited

FACING:
Hope springs eternal, and the Yankees had good reason to be optimistic for what was to come for Mantle (center) and teammates Hank Bauer (left) and Gene Woodling.

Photo by Hulton Archive/Getty Images

RIGHT:
A Mint-graded Mantle 1953 Bowman sold at auction for nearly $9,000 in April 2010.

Heritage Auction Galleries

A hit from either side of the plate, Mantle is photographed during mid-swing of his rookie year of 1951.

Heritage Auction Galleries

Superman in Pinstripes

In 1951 I was a small, skinny, shy dark-haired Jewish kid playing Little League on Long Island when Mick was called up by the Yankees and quickly became my favorite. With his power, speed, muscular build, and blond crew-cut, he seemed like a Superman descended from the heavens, not some shy kid from Oklahoma, of all places.

Even though Whitey Ford later came and made a promotional film at our Little League (and like me was a lefty and comparatively short), Mick remained my hero. When he came to the plate, there was always an extra element of excitement, because you never knew whether he would smash a colossal homer, drag a bunt for a base hit, or strike out like the mighty Casey.

— Steve Nelson, Washington, Massachusetts

There was great pressure on Mantle to succeed Joe DiMaggio as the next great Yankee. The media and many fans ridiculed him during his early struggles. Yet Mantle soon showed the baseball world that his future was bright and filled with promise.

Heritage Auction Galleries

Spring training 1952 was filled with promise for young Yankee hopefuls. From left,
outfielders Archie Wilson, Bob Cerv, Gene Woodling, Mickey Mantle, Jackie Jensen,
and Hank Bauer listen to manager Casey Stengel in St. Petersburg, Florida.

Kidwiler Collection/Diamond Images/Getty Images

Spring finally arrived, and Mantle reported to the Yankees' training camp in St. Petersburg, Florida, as one of two contenders for Joe DiMaggio's vacated centerfield spot. Joltin' Joe, 37 years old and coming off a .263, 12-homer season, had retired over the winter, hanging up his spikes due mainly to his nagging heel injury. Jackie Jensen was actually the favorite to earn the starting job in center; Mickey was coming off his knee surgery and the Yankees didn't know how well he had healed.

Mantle didn't start running close to full speed until two weeks into spring training. Stengel, not about to take any chances, eased Mantle into the lineup, alternating him in center with Jensen. When the season began, Jensen was in center, with Mantle flanking him in right. He went 3 for 4 that day, with a run and two RBI.

Mantle hit .304 the first week of the season, but Jensen started slowly, with only two hits in his first 19 at-bats. The Yankees quickly gave up on the right-handed-hitting Jensen, trading him to the Washington Senators for lefty-hitting centerfielder Iry Noren. (Jensen later won three RBI titles and the 1958 American League MVP award while playing for the Boston Red Sox)

Jensen's departure didn't immediately give the center field job to Mantle, who went into a minor slump at the plate. For two weeks after the trade, veterans Bob Cerv and Gene Woodling took turns in center. And then Mantle got his shot.

On May 20, the lineup card in a game against the Chicago White Sox read "Mantle, CF." He hit four singles that day, raising his average to .314. From there, he never looked back, finally putting himself on the path to replace Joe DiMaggio. A week later, he had another four-hit game, and then the power started coming: Mantle hit four homers in the second half of June, and nine in July.

He did it all with a heavy heart. Mutt Mantle died May 6, a victim of the same cancer that claimed other members of the Mantle family. He was 39. The loss of his father haunted Mickey for years.

There were other distractions, too. Mickey and Merlyn shared an apartment in New York with Billy Martin and his wife. Martin lived his life off the field the same way he played the game on the field—loud, flashy, and tough, with a wry sense of humor. He also liked to party, and the Mantle-Martin combination became legendary around New York and the American League.

The wisecracking city boy from the West Coast and country kid from the mining towns of Oklahoma hit it off from Day 1. Mantle admitted to living the high life, especially on road trips, where he and Billy tended to be the life of the party.

They were certainly the life of the party on the field. Martin's intensity and Mantle's bat helped lead the Yankees to their fourth straight pennant. Mickey, in his first full season in the majors, posted incredible numbers for a 20-year-old outfielder who had lost his father. He finished with a .311, 171 hits, 37 doubles, 87 RBI, and 23 homers. It started a string of 11 consecutive seasons in which he topped the 20-homer mark.

Defensively, Mantle tied for the American League lead in double plays, participating in five. But he also put up one statistic he'd just as soon forget; he led all outfielders with 14 errors.

In short order, though, Mantle improved as an outfielder. His speed allowed him to track down balls most players couldn't, and his arm was strong enough to throw out runners at any base. That combination of skills helped distinguish him as one of the finest center fielders in the game. Within two years, he would lead the league in assists with an impressive 25.

But it was at the plate where Mantle really shined. In the 1952 World Series, he was 10 for 29 (.345) against the Brooklyn Dodgers. He ripped two homers, scored five runs, and drove in three, helping the Yankees beat the Dodgers in seven games to capture their fourth straight World Series.

Both of Mantle's 1952 World Series homers were clutch hits. In Game 6, his 8th-inning homer gave the Yankees a 3-2 victory. In Game 7, his homer off Dodger rookie right-hander Joe Black in the 6th inning broke a 2-2 tie, giving the Yankees the lead for good.

Mantle's exploits in a Yankee uniform earned him a tribute he'd never envisioned. Shortly after the Yankees' World Series triumph, Mickey's hometown of Commerce honored him with a parade down Main Street. Hundreds of people lined the streets as Mickey and Merlyn waved and smiled from an open convertible. Later, a banquet followed in Mantle's honor.

No longer the brash newcomer, Mickey Mantle entered spring training of 1953 as the Yankees' regular center fielder. He also was the Yankees' offensive leader, so he was expected to carry a heavy share of the load as the Yankees took aim on an unprecedented fifth straight American League pennant and fifth consecutive World Series crown.

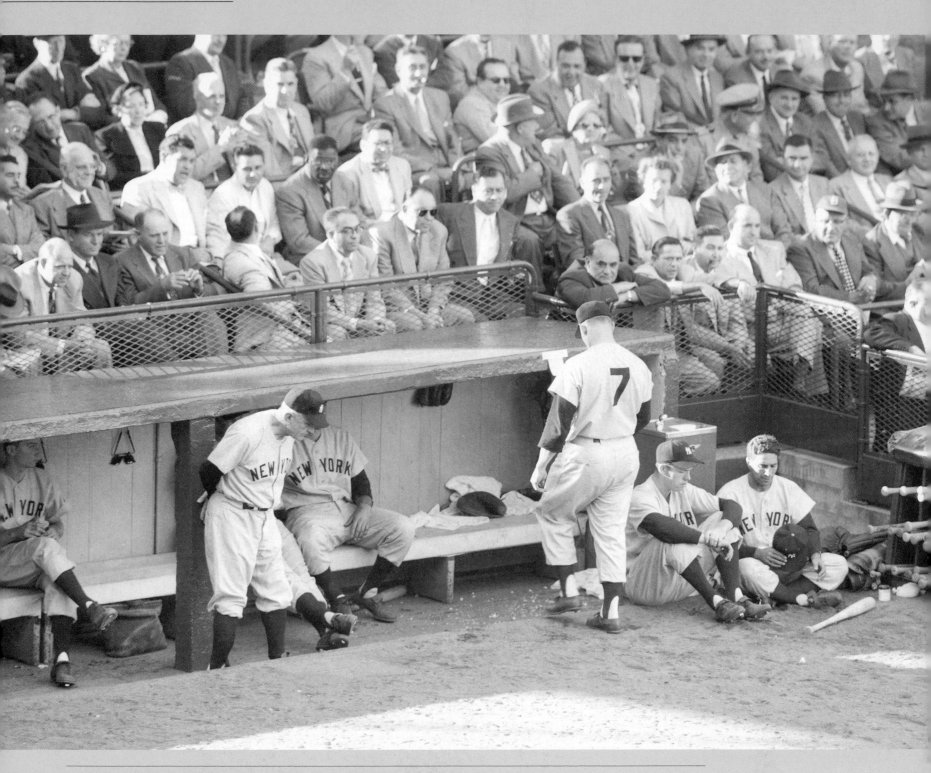

Baseball is a hit-and-miss kind of game, as Mantle discovered in game three of the 1953 World Series. After hitting the game-winning homer in game two, Mantle walks with head hung low after striking out for the fourth time in a 3-2 loss to the Brooklyn Dodgers. All manager Casey Stengel and others could do is look away and hope for better days. They wouldn't have to wait long as Mantle and the Yankees rebounded to win the series in six games. Mantle hit two home runs and drove in seven runs while striking out eight times in the series.

Photo by Charles Hoff/NY Daily News Archive via Getty Images

The Yankees were all smiles after Game 5 of the 1953 World Series against the Brooklyn Dodgers at Ebbets Field.
Jim McDonald (center) was the winning pitcher while the others all homered in the Yankees' 11-7 win. Shown
(clockwise from lower left) are Gil McDougald, Billy Martin, Mickey Mantle, Gene Woodling, and McDonald.

Photo by: Olen Collection/Diamond Images/Getty Images

MEMORIES OF MANTLE

Just a Minute, Mom...

I saw Mickey Mantle play often, but the thing I remember most was how many times in the mid-1950s that my mother had to hold up Sunday dinner because Mickey was on deck. I think millions of meals were held up because of No. 7.

The really amazing thing is that as good as Mickey Mantle was, he could never hit my stuff when I pitched against him in my mind or in my driveway with a tennis ball against the garage wall. Yogi, Roger, Moose, and the Scooter did no better, and Whitey Ford could never get a win against me, either, on Aster Road in West Islip on Long Island. I think it was the wind blowing in off the bay that affected their game...

— Howie Schneider, Orange Park, Florida

Mantle and Billy Martin became fast friends on the Yankees. The two quickly became well known for their play on and off the field. This autographed photo of the two outside the Hotel Edison sold for $567 at auction.

Heritage Auction Galleries

Mantle showed he could live up to those expectations in the final spring exhibition game. The Yankees, scheduled to play the Cincinnati Reds April 9, were then going to Pittsburgh to play the Pirates the next day. After the game against the Reds, Mickey, Billy Martin, and the third member of their good-time party-animal group, Whitey Ford, left by train for that well-known capital of suburban Cincinnati nightlife, Covington, Kentucky. The trio was supposed to be back at the station by 10 p.m. for the all-night ride to Pittsburgh, but they missed the train.

Plan B was to catch a plane for Pittsburgh, which would get them to the ballpark in plenty of time. But that night, a late winter storm moved in, and the resulting blizzard grounded all planes in the Cincinnati area. The trio's last hope was to convince a cabbie to drive them to Pittsburgh. A mere $500 and several hours later, the three arrived at the ballpark. Mantle and Martin missed batting practice, which angered Casey Stengel, who told the two exhausted ballplayers that they were going to play nine innings that day even if it killed them.

Despite the challenges of nightlife and travel, Mickey didn't have a bad day at all. In his first at bat, he crushed a ball that sailed clear over the right field stands—an estimated 550 feet.

Stengel couldn't argue with success or with a Ruthian shot (especially when it was hit under the classic Ruthian conditions of a near-sleepless night and attendant hangover), so he gave Mantle the rest of the day off.

That was only the first of a number of mammoth home runs to come in 1953. A week later, Mickey hit a ball that landed in the record books and inspired a new baseball term. The Yankees were playing the Washington Senators in Griffith Stadium when left-hander Chuck Stobbs served one up that Mantle hit just right. The ball not only went over the left-field fence, it cleared the bleachers and went halfway up the football scoreboard. It nicked the edge of a beer advertisement on the board and left the ballpark, landing across the street in someone's front yard.

After the game, Red Patterson, the Yankees' public relations man, grabbed a tape measure and paced off the distance of the blast. The figure he announced was 565 feet, longer and farther than any known home run in baseball history. The concept of the tape-measure home run was born.

Mantle missed a few games that year because of a mysterious rash. Shortly before the season, Merlyn gave birth to their first son, Mickey Elvin. The new dad developed an annoying rash that just wouldn't go away. It got so bad that Stengel told Mickey to go home to Oklahoma for a few days, see the baby, and relax, figuring the skin problem would clear up. Sure enough it did—on the flight home.

Mickey thought he should take a few days off anyway, so he went fishing. Naturally, a photographer snapped a picture of him with a fishing pole, looking relaxed and happy. He promptly received a phone call from New York telling him to get his rear end on the first plane out and to get back in uniform immediately.

For the rest of the season, the only ones getting nervous rashes were pitchers facing Mantle. His numbers weren't quite as outstanding as they were in 1952, but he played in 15 fewer games and had 89 fewer at-bats. Mickey wound up with 24 doubles, 21 homers, and 92 RBI. His average dropped to a still-impressive .295, and his slugging percentage was .497, down from the .530 he posted in 1952.

During the World Series, Mantle continued to shine. He homered in Game 2 as the Yankees jumped out to a commanding 2-0 lead over the Dodgers. Brooklyn manager Chuck Dressen's crew won the next two games, but in Game 5 Mickey ripped a grand slam in an 11-7 Yankee win that broke the Dodgers and paved the way for the Yankees' unprecedented fifth consecutive World Series.

During the winter of 1953-54, Mickey picked the wrong sport to occupy his time: basketball. He started working in a public relations role with Harold Youngman, a Kansas highway and asphalt contractor. Mickey's job was to make contacts and win road-paving contracts for Youngman's company. A bit bored with the constant schmoozing that went with his job, Mantle formed a basketball team named after Youngman's company.

With a few local athletic stars, among them his brothers Roy and Ray, Mantle began playing exhibition games, including a few against the Harlem Globetrotters. Things were just fine until Mickey, making a cut on a fast break, blew out his knee. He wound up in a Springfield, Missouri, hospital, where doctors removed some cartilage from his right knee—the same knee he damaged in the 1951 World Series.

Mantle left the hospital three days after the operation but never properly rehabilitated the knee. By spring training, he admitted he was still limping. And in favoring his good leg, he wound up with

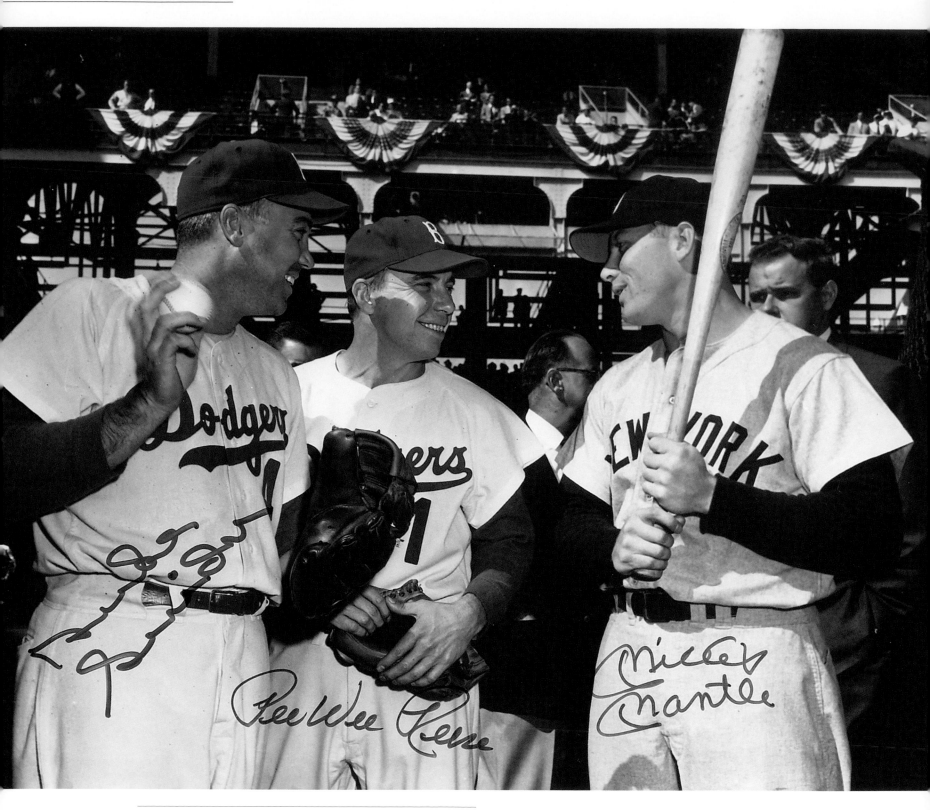

The Mick having a chat with Dodger all-time greats Duke Snider and Pee Wee Reese during their Yanks/Bums Subway Series in the mid-50s.

Photo courtesy of Heritage Auction Galleries

a strain in his left knee and muscle pulls and spasms elsewhere. His failure to properly rehabilitate himself after his two knee injuries, he later admitted, shortened his playing career by a matter of years, not weeks or months.

Meanwhile, Ray and Roy, who had just graduated from Commerce High, joined their big brother in the Yankees organization. Mickey, who thought they might have the necessary talent to succeed in the major league, persuaded Stengel to let them work out at Yankee Stadium. When the twins ripped liners during batting practice and impressed Stengel with their speed, the die was cast. Tom Greenwade, the same scout who signed Mickey, signed the twins, who were assigned to the Yankees' Class-D affiliate at McAllister, Oklahoma, in the Sooner State League.

Ray and Roy both hit over .300. They really opened eyes in Instructional League that winter; Roy hit over .400, while Ray outran everyone except Mickey. The twins moved up to Class C, but the story suddenly came to an unhappy ending when Roy injured his leg and Ray was drafted into the Army. Just like that, the possibility of an all-Mantle outfield—a thought that had some sportswriters in New York drooling over the headline possibilities—was over.

But Mickey was still around. Despite his injuries, the 22-year-old played in all but six games in 1954. For the first time, but not the last, he led the American League in runs scored (129) while posting double figures in doubles, triples, and homers. His 12 triples would be a career high, and his 27 home runs were his best power output to date. He also topped 100 RBIs (102) for the first time and coaxed his batting average back up to .300.

Those numbers were all right, but 1954 was the first time in six seasons the Yankees didn't win the pennant. The team played well, posting an impressive 103 victories (in fact, it was the first time in 13 seasons the Yanks exceeded the 100-win mark, and it was the highest total they'd ever amass under Stengel).

The problem was Al Lopez guided his Cleveland Indians to an amazing 111 wins, an American League record that would survive until the Yankees won 114 in 1998. (Three years later, the Seattle Mariners' topped that record with 116 wins.) While the Indians headed to the World Series (where they were swept by Willie Mays and the New York Giants), the Bronx Bombers went home to lick their wounds.

The Yankees returned to the World Series in 1955, a season in which Mickey Mantle offered a dress rehearsal of future greatness.

For the first time in his career, he won the AL home run title, blasting 37, and he added 11 triples (which tied him for the league lead) and 25 doubles. His .611 slugging percentage led the league, the first of four slugging titles he'd win.

Mantle also scored 121 runs, second best in the league, to go with 99 RBI and a .306 average. He put up these impressive numbers even though pitchers constantly pitched around him, as indicated by his league-leading 113 walks.

Although the Yankees reached the World Series, it wasn't their year. The Brooklyn Dodgers, weary of saying "Wait 'til next year," beat the Yankees in seven games, giving the borough of Brooklyn its only world title. The Series was frustrating for Mickey, whose injuries forced him to sit out the first two games, although his team won both.

Mantle did play in Game 3, hitting a solo home run off Johnny Podres, but the Yankees got hammered, 8-3. They lost Game 4, too, by an 8-5 score. Mickey's lone hit was a single.

At this point, Mantle's leg was bothering him so much that he appeared in only one more game, popping out as a pinch hitter against Podres in Game 7. He could only watch as the Dodgers won on Podres' eight-hit shutout, aided by Sandy Amoros' great catch to save at least two runs in the 6th inning. The Yankees headed into the winter quietly, but Mantle still managed to make some noise. The commissioner's office scheduled the Yankees to play an exhibition series in Japan against local professional teams. The trip was less appealing after the loss to the Dodgers, but everything was set. Most of the players brought their wives on the trip; Mickey and Billy Martin were exceptions.

After the novelty of sake (and perhaps the sushi) passed, Mantle tried desperately to find a way to get home. Merlyn was seven months pregnant, which kept her from making the trip to Japan. According to legend, long-time Mantle friend Harold Youngman suggested that someone back home send a telegram saying Merlyn was about to give birth and was having problems. It worked. The homesick outfielder was allowed to return to Oklahoma. Unfortunately, the commissioner's office later discovered that David Mantle wasn't born until December, making Mickey's ruse obvious. He drew a $5,000 fine—the amount he was paid for playing in Japan. Mickey didn't care, however. At that point, all he wanted to do was stay home, relax, and be with his growing family.

MEMORIES OF MANTLE

On the Way Up

In 1951, I was a baseball-mad boy of 13 growing up in northern California--with no TV. That spring, we all had heard of Mickey Mantle, but how would we watch him play? Fortunately, the Yankees made a rare West Coast pre-season swing in '51, so my dad took my brother and me down to Sacramento to see them play the Solons. Edmonds Park was full.

The initial sight of Mickey told you that he was like no other athlete. The first time he came up, he was batting left-handed and hit a ball over the high right-field wall at Edmonds. The second time up, batting right-handed, he hit a ball off the top of the wall in left.

Most of all, you noticed his speed --- it was like nothing we have seen, before or since. Back home, my friends just didn't believe me.

— John Holman, New York, N.Y.

This autographed photo montage shows Mantle, wearing No. 6, collecting his first career hit in his first game at Yankee Stadium in 1951. In his third at-bat, he broke through with a 6th-inning single off Boston's Bill Wight to drive in Phil Rizzuto. Mantle accumulated 2,415 career hits.

Heritage Auction Galleries

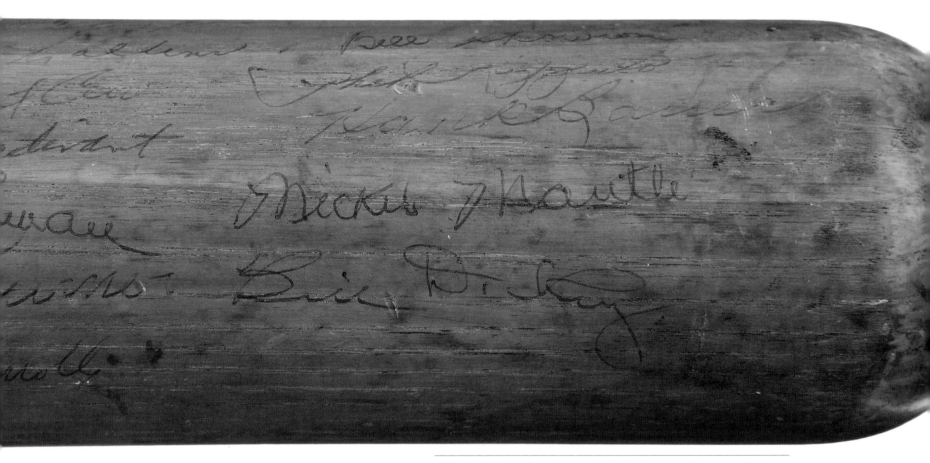

This 1955 game-used Mantle bat includes the signatures from 32 members from the 1955 Yankees team. The signature model Hillerich & Bradsby M110 matches Mantle's factory ordering records perfectly at 35 inches in length and 31 ounces. Mantle led the American League with a .611 slugging percentage and 37 home runs. A Mickey Mantle pro-model bat is one of the holy grails for an advanced bat, Mickey Mantle, Yankee memorabilia, or general historical baseball collection. For general collectors, a Mantle (or Ruth) bat is the ultimate Hall of Fame caliber baseball item, one that can be held and that provides a connection to the player in a way that all can appreciate, and one that transcends the world of sports collecting. The bat sold at Heritage Auction Galleries for $16,730 in April 2009.

1951

Regular Season

Year	Age	G	AB	R	H	2B	3B	HR	RB	SB	BB	SO	BA
1951	19	96	341	61	91	11	5	13	65	8	43	74	.267

World Series

Year	Age	G	AB	R	H	2B	3B	HR	RBI	SB	BB	SO	BA
1951	19	2	5	1	1	0	0	0	0	0	2	1	.200

Noteworthy

· On May 1, 1951, Mickey Mantle — wearing uniform No. 6 — connects for his first career major-league home run, a two-run blast in the 6th inning. The pitcher: right-hander Randy Gumpert of the Chicago White Sox.

· On July 13, the Yankees demote Mantle to the Double-A Kansas City Blues. At the time, he's hitting .261 with 7 HRs and 45 RBI.

· On Aug. 24, Mantle rejoins the Yankees. Clubhouse manager Pete Sheehy changes his uniform number from 6 to the 7 for which he becomes known. In his first 10 games back, he slugs four homers and drives in 11 runs.

1952

Regular Season

Year	Age	G	AB	R	H	2B	3B	HR	RBI	SB	BB	SO	BA
1952	20	142	549	94	171	37	7	23	87	4	75	111	.311

World Series

Year	Age	G	AB	R	H	2B	3B	HR	RBI	SB	BB	SO	BA
1952	20	7	29	5	10	1	1	2	3	0	3	4	.345

Noteworthy

· Mantle plays the season mourning the loss of his father, who dies of Hodgkin's Disease on May 6.

· On Oct. 6, he hits his first World Series homer. The Yankees win, 3-2, forcing a Game 7. Mantle also goes deep in that game, a 4-2 Yankees win.

1953

Regular Season

Year	Age	G	AB	R	H	2B	3B	HR	RBI	SB	BB	SO	BA
1953	21	127	461	105	136	24	3	21	92	8	79	90	.295

World Series

Year	Age	G	AB	R	H	2B	3B	HR	RBI	SB	BB	SO	BA
1953	22	6	24	3	5	0	0	2	7	0	3	8	.208

Noteworthy

· On April 17 at Griffith Stadium in Washington, D.C., Mantle (batting right-handed) hits a Chuck Stobbs pitch completely out of the park, prompting a PR man to walk off the distance. He measures it at 565 feet, giving rise to the "tape-measure home run."

· Mantle flexes his muscle in the Fall Classic by taking Preacher Roe deep for his first World Series homer (Game 2). In Game 5, he hits a memorable grand slam.

1954

Regular Season

Year	Age	G	AB	R	H	2B	3B	HR	RBI	SB	BB	SO	BA
1954	22	146	543	129	163	17	12	27	102	5	102	107	.267

Noteworthy

· Mantle surpasses the 100-RBI mark for the first time.

· Mantle serves notice to opposing base runners by notching 20 outfield assists.

1955

Regular Season

Year	Age	G	AB	R	H	2B	3B	HR	RBI	SB	BB	SO	BA
1955	23	147	517	121	158	25	11	37	99	8	113	97	.306

World Series

Year	Age	G	AB	R	H	2B	3B	HR	RBI	SB	BB	SO	BA
1955	23	3	10	1	2	0	0	1	1	0	0	2	.200

Noteworthy

· The Mick enjoys his first three-homer game, on May 13. He also hits a single, giving him a 4-for-4 game, and drives in all of the Yankees' runs in a 5-2 win over Detroit.

· On July 9, Mantle notches his first five-hit game in a 14-9 win over Washington.

· Mantle's stats in 1955 include league-leading figures in homers, walks, and slugging percentage (.611).

· On Sept. 30, he hits his fifth World Series homer, although the Yankees ultimately lose the championship to the Dodgers.

An early shot of The Mick holding two bats, signifying his talent as a switch hitter. No switch hitter in Major League history drilled them out of the park than Mantle.

Heritage Auction Galleries

Mantle could be found everywhere you turned in that magical summer of '56. His appearance on the cover of *Life* magazine on June 25 was just about the biggest tribute a ballplayer could receive. This signed copy of the magazine sold for $420 at auction.

Heritage Auction Galleries

Blessed with rare speed for a power hitter, Mantle hit 22
doubles and five triples in 1956. He also had 10 stolen bases.

Photo by Ralph Morse//Time Life Pictures/Getty Images

Yankees' manager Casey Stengel helps Mantle celebrate his Triple Crown season. The 16 x 20-inch image is boldly autographed by Mantle.

Heritage Auction Galleries

One-Man Gang

I personally relish "perfect moments" and like so many others, I have lots of "Mickey moments." Many of them aren't specific homers or plays, either. Here's a rather subtle one (actually, it happened several times, according to my memory): After a Mickey solo homer early in a game gave the Yanks the lead, Red Barber broke for a commercial by saying, "Mickey 1, White Sox 0."

There's a line from Bruce Springsteen's song "Racing in the Streets" that says, "I want to blow 'em all out of their seats..." Well, no athlete that I've ever seen (and I've seen them all since 1955, when I was 5) automatically brought everybody to the edge of their seats in anticipation the way Mickey did.

— Evan Gary Wolgang, Manhattan Beach, Calif.

Mantle's Triple Crown Award (along with the personal message from Mantle) sold for $211,500 in the 1999 Barry Halper Auction in New York. Halper, who died in 2005, had one of the finest collections of baseball memorabilia in the world.

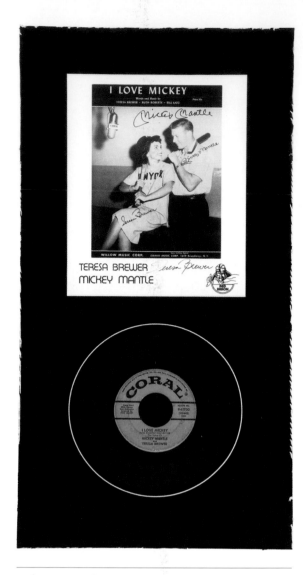

In the summer of 1956, singing sensation Teresa Brewer performed the memorable song "I Love Mickey" as a testament to the fabulous playing style of Yankees star Mickey Mantle. Here is a glossy 8 x 10-inch image of both the young Yankees superstar and the popular singer plus an original 45 rpm record of the hit song.

Rawlings hit a home run with kids when it brought Mantle on board to sell its baseball gloves. With The Mick on its team, Rawlings certainly was "The Finest in The Field."

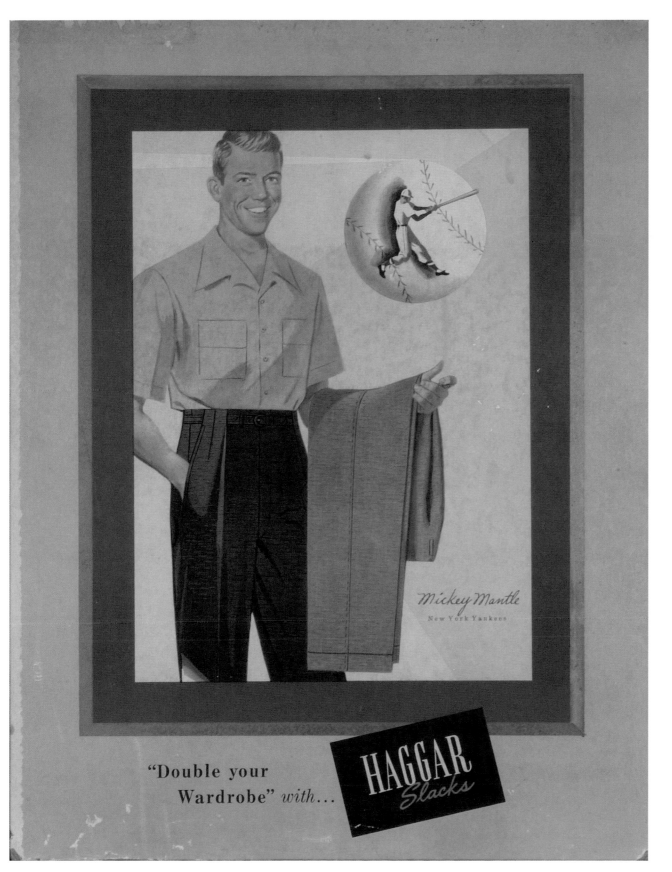

"Double your Wardrobe" with... **HAGGAR** *Slacks*

Beginning in 1954 and continuing until the 1960s, the Dallas, Texas-based Haggar Slacks Co. used Mantle as one of its primary spokesmen, along with Arnold Palmer, Bobby Layne and others. Haggar's ads appeared regularly in *Sports Illustrated*, *Sport* and other top-selling magazines. This bright and colorful cardboard counter display (14 x 18.75 inches) is an extremely rare piece and stands today as a prime example of 1950s Americana. It sold for nearly $4,000 at a Robert Edward Auctions sale.

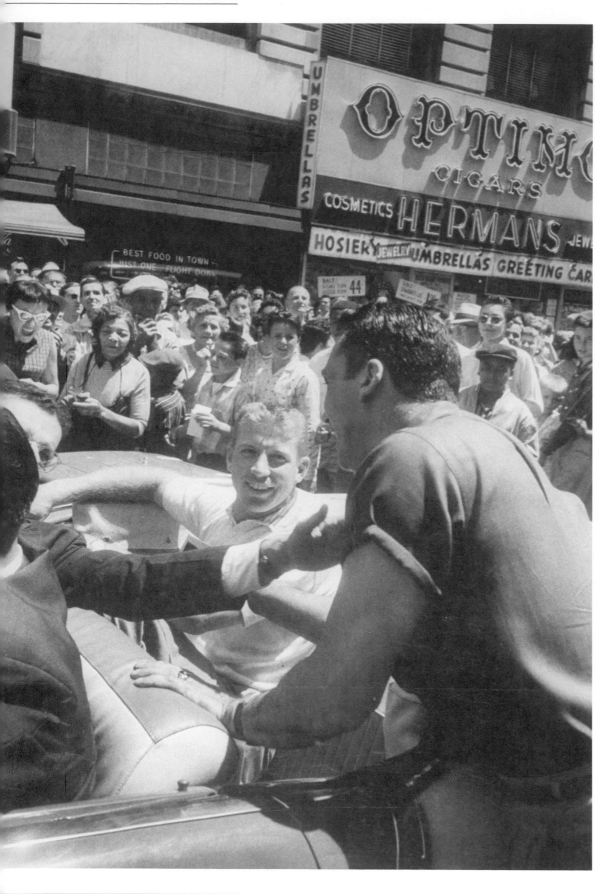

ABOVE:

As Mantle's popularity increased so did the demand on his time. As his son Mickey Jr. waits, Mantle autographs a stack of photographs for fans.

Ralph Morse//Time Life Pictures/Getty Images

LEFT:

Fans press in around Mickey Mantle as the Yankee great travels in a player motorcade through the streets of New York.

Ralph Morse//Time Life Pictures/Getty Images

When your goal is to win the Triple Crown you take good care of your lumber. Here Mantle "bones" his bat while his Rawlings model fielder's glove rests on his knee prior to a game at Yankee Stadium. Players used a cow bone nailed to a piece of wood to "bone" or compress the grain on the barrel of their baseball bats to harden the wood and make it less likely to chip.

Heritage Auction Galleries

1957-1960: Prime Mantle

FACING:

New York Yankees Mickey Mantle, Billy Martin, Hank Bauer, and Bauer's wife Charlene leaving the district attorney's office June 25, 1957, after a grand jury declined to indict Bauer on charges of assault that stemmed from "The Brawl at the Copa." Despite the "victory," the Yankees dumped Martin, who they considered a troublemaker and a bad influence on Mantle, trading him to Kansas City.

Bob Costello/NY Daily News Archive via Getty Images

IN 1956, MICKEY MANTLE DREW RAVES FROM ALL CORNERS. His speed impressed Ted Williams just as much as his power. "If I could run like Mantle, I'd hit .400 every year," said The Splendid Splinter, who lost the batting race to Mantle, .353 to .348, on the last day of the season. And then there was manager Casey Stengel's classic quote: "He should lead the league in everything. With his combination of speed and power he should win the triple batting crown every year. In fact, he should do anything he wants to do."

Well, it wasn't quite that easy. Mantle would never "put it all together" again like he did in 1956. Even so, he continued slugging home runs, scoring runs, driving in runs, and hitting for average with the best in baseball. And he did it despite injuries on the field and tough times off the field.

The 1957 season, for example, provided its share of turmoil for Mantle. The most famous incident involving the star center fielder happened on May 15. Mickey, Whitey Ford, Hank Bauer, Yogi Berra, and Johnny Kucks, all with their wives, arranged a birthday party for Billy Martin. The six couples met for dinner and went to the famed Copacabana nightclub in New York to watch Sammy Davis Jr.

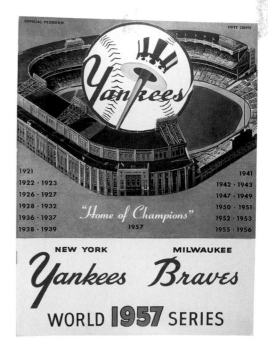

Program for the 1957 World Series pitting the Yankees against the Milwaukee Braves.

Billy Martin and Mantle were great friends, but the hot-tempered Martin proved to be a combustible teammate as well. The Yankees finally tired of him in 1957, trading him to Kansas City. But the organization could not stay angry at the fiery Martin: he returned to the team in 1975 for the first of five stints as Yankee manager. This autographed picture of Martin sold for $150 at a Heritage Auction Galleries sale.

COPYRIGHT ©1987 HISTORIC LIMITED EDITIONS - WILLISTON PARK, NEW YORK   LIMITED SERIES #1

While Mickey Mantle and Whitey Ford would play their entire careers for the New York Yankees and end up in the Baseball Hall of Fame, their friend Billy Martin bounced around the league after being traded to Kansas City. Martin played one season with Kansas City, batting .257 in 73 games. In the following years he would play for Detroit, Cleveland, Cincinnati, Milwaukee, and Minnesota. This signed lithograph by artist Susan Rini was part of the Whitey Ford Collection.

Heritage Auction Galleries

Walk-Off Magic

It was June 18, 1959, and my Aunt Mary, an avid Yankees fan, took a few of my cousins and me to the Stadium. It was an afternoon game, but we got parental "dispensation" to skip school. I was 11, and this was the first time I attended a major league game. The Yankees were playing the White Sox and the score was tied, 4-4, in the bottom of the 10th inning. And then The Mick came up—and ended it with a game-winning homer!

It was an unbelievable day for me: I went to my first game and saw my boyhood idol hit not just a home run, but the game-winner.

— Steve Soricelli, Enfield, Connecticut

Reporters surround Mantle after he hit two home runs in the World Series against the Pirates, October 1, 1960. Mantle was a monster in the Series. He collected 10 hits, three homers, 11 RBI, and a .400 average. It was his best World Series, but the Yankees lost in seven games.

Art Rickerby//Time Life Pictures/Getty Images

RBI), plus rookie Tony Kubek, who hit .297 in 127 games while playing five positions. The Yankees surged to their eighth pennant in nine years and faced off against the upstart Milwaukee Braves in the World Series. After finishing just one game behind the N.L. Champion Brooklyn Dodgers in 1956, the Braves won their first pennant since moving to Milwaukee from Boston in 1953. Milwaukee's lineup featured sluggers Hank Aaron (.322, 44 homers, 132 RBI) and Eddie Mathews (.292, 32, 94), and their rotation included Warren Spahn, Lew Burdette, and Bob Buhl, who had a combined 56-27 record.

The Yankees and Braves split the first two games in New York, with the Yanks winning Game 1 3-1 and the Braves winning Game 2 4-2. The action then moved to Milwaukee for a crucial Game 3 matchup. It was during that game that a fluke play turned the Series and made a significant impact on Mantle's career.

Kubek, a Milwaukee native, homered in the first inning off the Brave's Bob Buhl. Mantle and Berra followed with walks. Mantle took a large lead off second, hoping to help the Yankees blow the game open. Buhl threw wildly to second trying to keep Mantle close. Mantle dove headfirst into the bag;. Milwaukee second baseman Red Schoendienst, in going after the ball, slipped and landed on Mantle's shoulder. Mickey pushed Schoendienst away and moved to third on the play as the Braves's outfielders chased down the ball. Mantle finished the game and the Yankees would go on to win, 12-3, but that play had big implications on the Series. Mantle's shoulder stiffened overnight. The shoulder got so painful that Mantle pulled himself during the 10th inning of Game 4, which the Yankees lost 7-5. Because of his bum shoulder, Mantle did not play in the field in Game 5 and Game 6, which the teams split. In the deciding Game 7, Mantle played but collected only a single in four at bats. The Braves, behind the brilliant pitching of Lew Burdette, won the game 5-0 and their first World Series since "the Miracle Braves" of 1914. Burdette was named World Series MVP after pitching three complete games and two shutouts, becoming the first pitcher since the legendary Christy Mathewson in 1905 to pitch two shutouts in World Series play.

Although Mantle did not match the numbers of his Triple Crown season, you could argue that he was just as dominant. Mantle led the league in runs and walks and batted a career-high .365. He also hit into a league-low five double plays. Furthermore, Mantle reached base more times than he made outs (319-312), one of two

seasons in which he accomplished the feat. Along the way Mantle won his second straight MVP award.

Still, things were not great in New York. After the season, Yankee GM Weiss sent Mantle a contract calling for a $5,000 pay cut. Weiss reasoned that Mantle's statistics—the .365 average, 34 home runs, 94 RBI, and 121 runs scored, with 16 stolen bases to boot—weren't as good as those in 1956. That, coupled with the Yankees' World Series loss, likely weighed heavily on his offer.

Miffed, Mantle refused to show up for spring training in St. Petersburg, Florida, in February 1958. Weiss told reporters that he would handle the situation by doing the unthinkable: trading Mantle. But few believed Weiss' bluff. When Mantle finally showed up, however, he had a new contract with a $12,500 pay raise. As it turned out, the contract dustup was the least of Mantle's worries.

The 1958 season started oddly for New Yorkers. Both the Dodgers and the Giants had moved to California (Los Angeles and San Francisco, respectively) leaving only the Yankees to cheer for. Mantle had undergone surgery in the off-season, but his shoulder gave him problems throughout spring. As the season unfolded, he started slowly, although his team did not. The Yankees won 23 of their first 28 games and never looked back, ultimately winning the pennant by 10 games over the White Sox.

By season's end, Mantle's numbers had rebounded. For the fourth time, he led the league in runs scored (127), and for the third time, he led the league in walks (129). He also won his third home run title (42) while pacing the league in total bases for the second time (307). He hit a solid .304 and drove in 97 runs, fifth best in the league. Not surprisingly, the Yankees won their third straight pennant and earned a rematch against the Braves in the World Series.

Milwaukee won three of the first four games of the Series and seemed poised to win its second straight championship. But the Yankees swept the final three games—the last two in Milwaukee —to win their sixth World Series crown of the decade and fifth since Mantle joined the ballclub. In winning the championship, the Yankees became only the second team in Major League Baseball history to come back from a 3-1 deficit to win a best-of-seven World Series. The Pittsburgh Pirates turned the trick in 1925. For his part, Mantle had a triple, two homers, and three runs batted in during the Series.

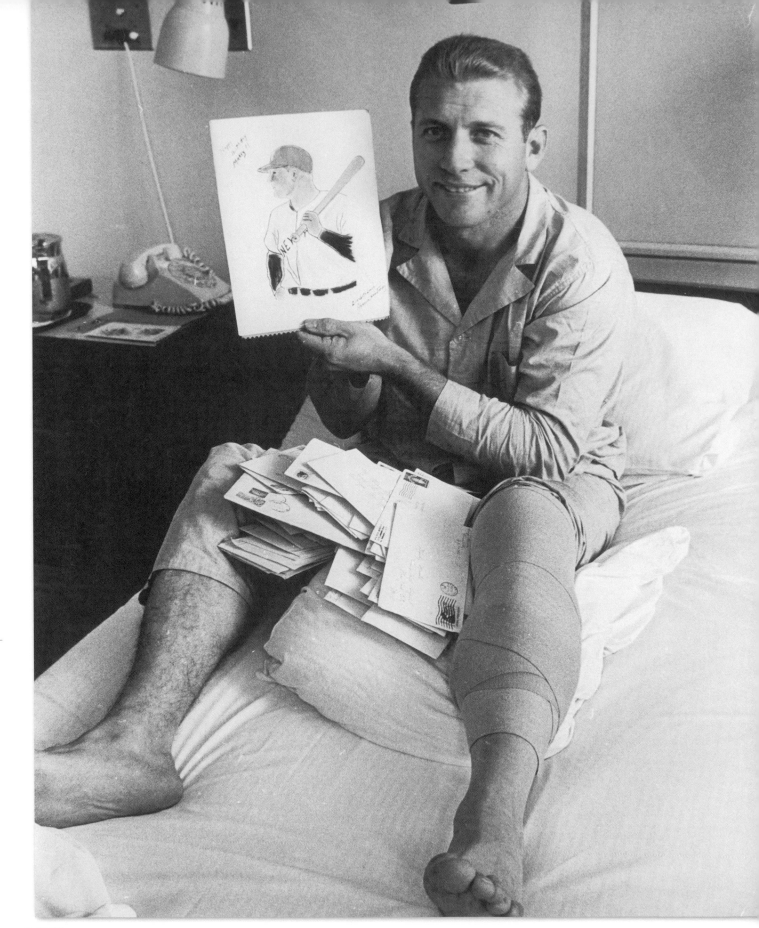

Despite the leg injuries that cut his career short, Mantle emerged as one of the most beloved athletes of his or any generation. Here, he sits on a bed in his pajamas, his left leg wrapped in bandages and elevated on a pillow, with a stack of fan mail on his lap while holding a portrait of himself sent by a fan as a birthday card.

Bruce Bennett Studios/Getty Images

The good feelings soured during the World Series against the Pittsburgh Pirates. Game 1 turned out to be crucial, not only for the Yankees, but for Stengel's future. Casey passed on Whitey Ford and started Art Ditmar in the opener at Pittsburgh's Forbes Field. As with all controversial moves, managers are either heroes or bums. This time, Stengel wound up a bum; the Pirates hammered Ditmar and won the opener, 6-4.

Yankee sluggers dominated the next two games, ripping Pirate pitching for 16-3 and 10-0 victories, the latter a four-hit shutout by Ford at Yankee Stadium. The Pirates then swept the next two games in the Bronx, 3-2 and 5-2, meaning the Yankees had to win the final two games, both at Forbes Field.

In Game 6, Ford did his best to keep the Yankees alive. He tossed his second shutout of the Series in a 12-0 win. In Game 7, the Pirates jumped to a 4-0 lead after two innings, but Skowron and Berra homered, giving the Yankees a 5-4 lead. It was 7-4 in the 8th inning when a potential double-play grounder took a bad hop, striking shortstop Tony Kubek in the throat. Kubek was badly hurt and forced to leave the game.

Given new life, the Pirates rallied for five runs, the big blow a three-run homer by backup catcher Hal Smith. Suddenly, the Yankees were down 9-7 going into the 9th inning. Bobby Richardson and Dale Long both singled, bringing Mantle to the plate. Mickey ripped a single off lefty Harvey Haddix (his 10th hit of the Series) to drive in Richardson (his 11th RBI). Berra then drove home the tying run, keeping the Yankees' title hopes alive—for a few moments.

In the bottom of the 9th, the Pirates' Bill Mazeroski sent Ralph Terry's second pitch of the inning high over the ivy-covered left field wall. The Pirates won, 10-9, capturing an improbable World Series. The image of Mazeroski hopping around the base paths as his teammates roared out of the dugout to celebrate is one of the most enduring images in baseball history, much to the Yankees' chagrin.

Statistically, the Yankees had dominated. They batted an astounding .338 with 11 home runs and 55 runs scored in seven games. By comparison, the Pirates hit just .256 with only 26 runs and four homers. Pittsburgh's pitchers posted some ugly numbers, too, including a 7.11 ERA. Four of their pitchers had ERAs higher than 10.

MEMORIES OF MANTLE

A Perfect Sunday

I have memories of Mickey Mantle on the late-1950s television show *Home Run Derby*, and of how humble he seemed. I guess it was more a matter of the discomfort he felt in discussing himself than humbleness, but for a kid, it was all the same.

Beginning in 1960, I was really into baseball—I mean it was all I thought about. And 1961 was heaven. The perfect Sunday was taking a subway from Far Rockaway to the Stadium, sitting in the grandstand, and watching batting practice followed by a doubleheader. We paid 60 cents for the subway (the Rockaway line was a double fare in those days) and $1.30 for the seats. Of course, if Mantle was out, it wasn't worth the trip. He was the one that you paid to watch.

I remember the shot that Mantle hit off Bill Fischer that hit the top of the facade [May 22, 1963] and came as close to going out of Yankee Stadium as any ball that I ever saw. It was majestic, and the newspaper pictures the next day traced the flight of the ball.

I watched every Mantle at-bat waiting for the inevitable moment that he would succeed and clear the roof. To me, as a kid, it wasn't if, it was when. The other sluggers of the day were, to me, home run hitters, but Mantle was a power hitter.

I also remember going to Mantle's last home game— and feeling the disappointment at how empty Yankee Stadium was that day.

— Marc J. Sicklick, Cedarhurst, N.Y.

[Ed. Note: Mantle's last game at Yankee Stadium was on Sept. 25, 1968. He started at first base, batted third, and played the entire game, going 1 for 3 with a walk and two strikeouts. The Yankees lost to Cleveland, 3-0, on a one-hit shutout by Luis Tiant. The only Yankee hit: a Mantle single to the center. The attendance that day: 5,723.]

Mantle was a monster in the Series. He collected 10 hits, three homers, 11 RBI, and a .400 average. It was his best World Series, but the Yankees lost. Even worse for Mantle, the Yanks, by his estimation, lost to a less-talented team that they had outplayed.

Two days after the Series ended, so did the Casey Stengel era. The Yankees fired Stengel, saying that at 70 years of age, he just didn't have it anymore. Stengel's rebuke: "Most people are dead at

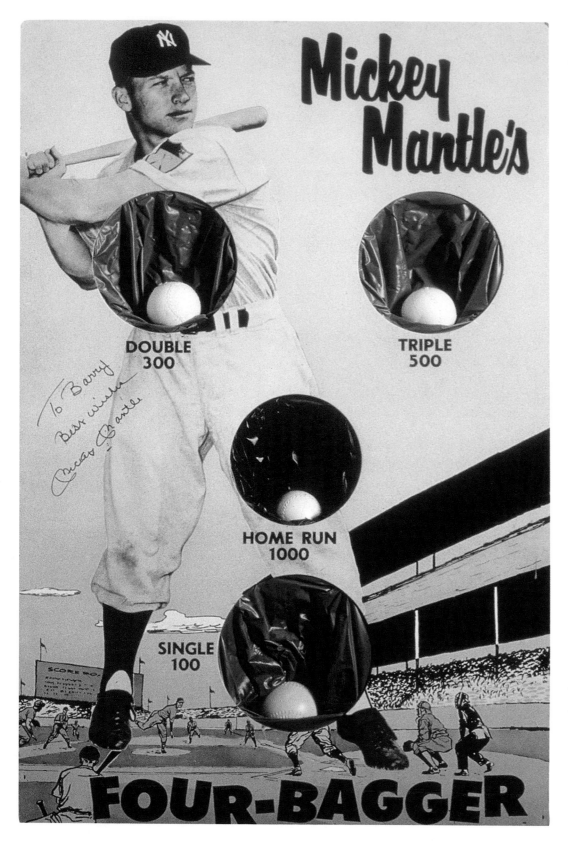

The Mickey Mantle Four-Bagger was one of the first games to feature Mantle. Three different versions of the game were created. The standard game measured 22 x 34 inches and came with four "ultron" pockets and three rubber balls. The object: throw the balls into one of the pockets for points. A single was worth 100 points; a double 200; a triple 500; and a home run 1,000. The game board featured a colorful, lifelike figure of Mickey batting at the plate. The game also had a heavy wire easel that prevented it from easily tipping over. The suggested retail price: $5.

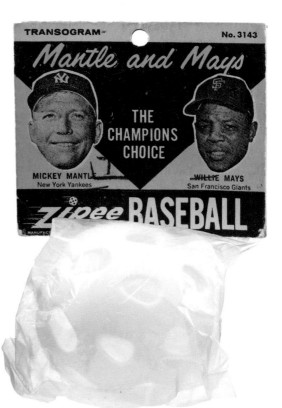

One of the many toys Mantle endorsed was this 1960s Transogram Whiffle ball (also endorsed by Willie Mays).

Heritage Auction Galleries.

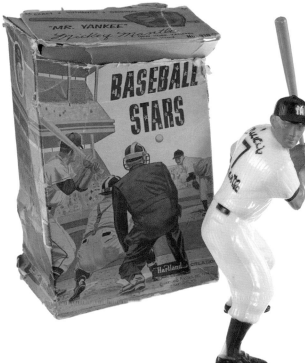

From 1958 through 1963, Hartland Plastics of Hartland, Wisconsin, produced 18 different 8-inch Major League Baseball players, including Mickey Mantle, who was shown batting left-handed. The lifelike statues retailed for $1.98 and came in their own individual boxes. The statue also featured a nametag that hung around the player's neck.

The Hartland Statues have long been a popular item in the sports memorabilia hobby and probably served as the inspiration for an entire hobby niche of figurine collecting. The Mantle piece is one of the keys to the 18-player set. The original Mantle box and name tag are sought-after items in the collecting market, as most were discarded by kids just wanting to play with the statues. Values for empty original boxes and tags can range from $150-$400 depending on condition. This autographed statue sold for $1,075 at auction.

Heritage Auction Galleries

Released in the late 1950s, Zoom Ball was a great toy that taught youngsters how to throw and catch, while helping develop hand-eye coordination. The toy featured a white Mickey Mantle stamped signature rubber ball attached to a long rubber band that attached to the thrower's glove. When thrown or "zoomed," the ball would come back quickly. Sometimes too quickly. The result could be a Zoom Ball in the face. The game was pulled from the market after a short run. The Zoom Ball's original price was $1 and it was made by Toplay Products Inc., New York, N.Y.

UNIFORM PLAYER'S CONTRACT

American League of Professional Baseball Clubs

Parties   Between   NEW YORK YANKEES
herein called the Club, and   Mickey C. Mantle
of   Commerce, Oklahoma , herein called the Player.

Recital   The Club is a member of the American League of Professional Baseball Clubs, a voluntary association of eight member clubs which has subscribed to the Major League Rules with the National League of Professional Baseball Clubs and its constituent clubs and to the Major-Minor League Rules with that League and the National Association of Baseball Leagues. The purpose of those rules is to insure the public wholesome and high-class professional baseball by defining the relations between Club and Player, between club and club, between league and league, and by vesting in a designated Commissioner broad powers of control and discipline, and of decision in case of disputes.

Agreement   In consideration of the facts above recited and of the promises of each to the other, the parties agree as follows:

Employment   1. The Club hereby employs the Player to render, and the Player agrees to render, skilled services as a baseball player during the year 195_7_ including the Club's training season, the Club's exhibition games, the Club's playing season, and the World Series (or any other official series in which the Club may participate and in any receipts of which the player may be entitled to share).

Payment   2. For performance of the Player's services and promises hereunder the Club will pay the Player the sum of $60,000.00, as follows:

In semi-monthly installments after the commencement of the playing season covered by this contract, unless the Player is "abroad" with the Club for the purpose of playing games, in which event the amount then due shall be paid on the first week-day after the return "home" of the Club, the terms "home" and "abroad" meaning respectively at and away from the city in which the Club has its baseball field.

If a monthly rate of payment is stipulated above, it shall begin with the commencement of the Club's playing season (or such subsequent date as the Player's services may commence) and end with the termination of the Club's scheduled playing season, and shall be payable in semi-monthly installments as above provided.

If the player is in the service of the Club for part of the playing season only, he shall receive such proportion of the sum above mentioned, as the number of days of his actual employment in the Club's playing season bears to the number of days in said season.

If the rate of payment stipulated above is less than $6,000 per year, the player, nevertheless, shall be paid at the rate of $6,000 for each day of his service as a player on a Major League team.

Loyalty   3. (a) The Player agrees to perform his services hereunder diligently and faithfully, to keep himself in first class physical condition and to obey the Club's training rules, and pledges himself to the American public and to the Club to conform to high standards of personal conduct, fair play and good sportsmanship.

Baseball Promotion   (b) In addition to his services in connection with the actual playing of baseball, the Player agrees to cooperate with the Club and participate in any and all promotional activities of the Club and its League, which, in the opinion of the Club, will promote the welfare of the Club or professional baseball, and to observe and comply with all requirements of the Club respecting conduct and service of its teams and its players, at all times whether on or off the field.

Pictures and Public Appearances   (c) The Player agrees that his picture may be taken for still photographs, motion pictures or television at such times as the Club may designate and agrees that all rights in such pictures shall belong to the Club and may be used by the Club for publicity purposes in any manner it desires. The Player further agrees that during the playing season he will not make public appearances, participate in radio or television programs or permit his picture to be taken or write or sponsor newspaper or magazine articles or sponsor commercial products without the written consent of the Club, which shall not be withheld except in the reasonable interests of the Club or professional baseball.

Player Representations   4. (a) The Player represents and agrees that he has exceptional and unique skill and ability as a baseball player; that his services to be rendered hereunder are of a special, unusual and extraordinary character which gives them peculiar value which cannot be reasonably or adequately compensated for in damages at law, and that the Player's breach of this contract will cause the Club great and irreparable injury and damage. The Player therefore agrees that, in addition to other remedies, the Club shall be entitled to injunctive and other equitable relief to prevent a breach of this contract by the Player, including, among others, the right to enjoin the Player from playing baseball for any other person or organization during the term of this contract.

Ability

Condition   (b) The Player represents that he has no physical or mental defects, known to him, which would prevent or impair performance of his services.

Interest in Club   (c) The Player represents that he does not, directly or indirectly, own stock or have any financial interest in the ownership or earnings of any Major League club, except as hereinafter expressly set forth, and covenants that he will not hereafter, while connected with any Major League club, acquire or hold any such stock or interest except in accordance with Major League Rule 20 (e).

Service   5. (a) The Player agrees that, while under contract, and prior to expiration of the Club's right to renew this contract, he will not play baseball otherwise than for the Club, except that the Player may participate in post-season games under the conditions prescribed in the Major League Rules. Major League Rule 18 (b) is set forth on page 4 hereof.

(2) Upon receipt of the waiver request, any other Major League club may claim assignment of this contract at a waiver price of $1.00, the priority of claims to be determined in accordance with the Major League Rules.

(3) If this contract is so claimed, the Club shall, promptly and before any assignment, notify the Player that it had requested waivers for the purpose of terminating this contract and that the contract has been claimed.

(4) Within 5 days after receipt of notice of such claim, the Player shall be entitled, by written notice to the Club, to terminate this contract on the date of his notice of termination. If the Player fails so to notify the Club, this contract shall be assigned to the claiming club.

(5) If the contract is not claimed, the Club shall promptly deliver written notice of termination to the Player at the expiration of the waiver period.

Upon any termination of this contract by the Player, all obligations of both parties hereunder shall cease on the date of termination, except the obligation of the Club to pay the Player's compensation to ...

The Player accepts as part of this contract the Regulations printed on the fourth page hereof.

... The Club and the Player agree to accept, abide by and comply with all provisions of the Major-Minor League Rules which concern player conduct and player-club relationships and with all ... of the Commissioner and the President of the Club's League, pursuant thereto.

... case of dispute between the Player and the Club, the same shall be referred to the Commissioner ... arbitrator, and his decision shall be accepted by all parties as final; and the Club and the Player agree ... such dispute, or any claim or complaint by either party against the other, shall be presented to the ... sioner within one year from the date it arose.

The Club, the League President and the Commissioner, or any of them, may make public the findings, ... and record of any inquiry, investigation or hearing held or conducted, including in such record all ... or information, given, received or obtained in connection therewith.

(a) On or before January 15 (or if a Sunday, then the next preceding business day) of the year ... owing the last playing season covered by this contract, the Club may tender to the Player a contract ... term of that year by mailing the same to the Player at his address following his signature hereto, or if ... given, then at his last address of record with the Club. If prior to the March 1 next succeeding said ... 15, the Player and the Club have not agreed upon the terms of such contract, then on or before 10 ... or said March 1, the Club shall have the right by written notice to the Player at said address to renew ... tract for the period of one year on the same terms, except that the amount payable to the Player shall ... as the Club shall fix in said notice; provided, however, that said amount, if fixed by a Major League ... all be an amount payable at a rate not less than 75% of the rate stipulated for the preceding year.

The Club's right to renew this contract, as provided in subparagraph (a) of this paragraph 10, ... promise of the Player not to play otherwise than with the Club have been taken into consideration ... mining the amount payable under paragraph 2 hereof.

This contract is subject to federal or state legislation, regulations, executive or other official orders ... governmental action, now or hereafter in effect respecting military, naval, air or other governmental ... which may directly or indirectly affect the Player, Club or the League and subject also to the right ... commissioner to suspend the operation of this contract during any national emergency.

The term "Commissioner" wherever used in this contract shall be deemed to mean the Commissioner ... ed under the Major League Agreement, or in the case of a vacancy in the office of Commissioner, ... cutive Council or such other body or person or persons as shall be designated in the Major League ... nt to exercise the powers and duties of the Commissioner during such vacancy.

Club and the Player covenant that this contract fully sets forth all understandings and agreements ... them, and agree that no other understandings or agreements, whether heretofore or hereafter made, ... valid, recognizable, or of any effect whatsoever, unless expressly set forth in a new or supplemental ... executed by the Player and the Club (acting by its president, or such other officer as shall have ... hereunto duly authorized by the president or Board of Directors, as evidenced by a certificate filed of record with the League President and Commissioner) and complying with the Major and Major-Minor League Rules.

Special Covenants

Approval   This contract or any supplement hereto shall not be valid or effective unless and until approved by the League President.

Signed in duplicate this _6th_ day of _February_, A. D. 195_7_

Mickey Mantle (Player)   _New York Yankees_ (Club)

(Home address of Player)   By _____ (Authorized Signature)

Social Security No. _____

Approved _____, 195___

President, American League of Professional Baseball Clubs

Mantle playfully hits a snowball February 4, 1957, in Yankee Stadium after signing his contract (above) for the upcoming season. The '57 season would be another smash for Mantle, who hit .365 with 34 home runs, 94 runs driven in, 121 runs scored, and 16 stolen bases. He also was walked a league-leading 146 times. At the end of the season Mantle was named the American League Most Valuable Player for the second time in his career.

Guernsey's

The Big Three of baseball royalty—Ted Williams, Stan Musical, and Mickey Mantle—appear on *The Steve Allen Show* with "Salute to Baseball in 1957."

Yale Joel//Time Life Pictures/Getty Images

Mantle won his second Most Valuable Player award in 1957. The prestigious award, named after Kennesaw Mountain Landis, the first commissioner of baseball, sold for $319,250 at auction in 2003.

Guernsey's

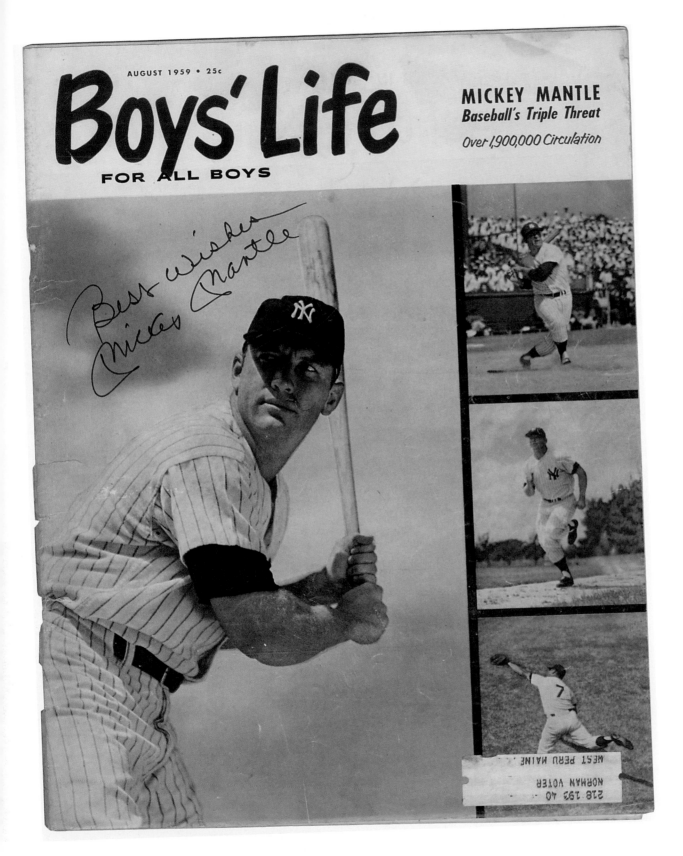

In the midst of the 1959 season, Mantle graced the cover of the August issue of *Boys' Life*. The season was kind neither to Mantle nor the Yankees. Mickey batted .285 with 31 home runs and 75 runs batted in. The Yankees finished in third place with a 79-75 record. But all of that was to change in the off-season in one of the most important trades in the club's history. In a seven-player deal with the Kansas City Athletics, the Yankees acquired Roger Maris, and the fortunes of the team and Mantle changed dramatically. This Mantle-autographed magazine sold for more than $300 at auction.

Heritage Auction Galleries

Actor and comedian Billy Crystal paid $239,000 for what was believed to be a 1960 "circa" Mickey Mantle glove. Crystal bought the glove in 1999 during the famous "Barry Halper Collection of Baseball Memorabilia" at Sotheby's. The Rawlings glove was autographed by Mantle and said to have been made exclusively for him. In an interview on *60 Minutes* after the purchase, Crystal said he rests the glove on a seat from Yankee Stadium inscribed by his hero: "Wish you were still sitting here and I was still playing." Crystal said in the interview: "Every day, I walk by it and I either put the glove on or just look at it. And it just puts me in touch with something good. And I always feel good that I have it." Crystal served as the director and executive producer of the highly acclaimed 2001 HBO film *61**, the story of Mantle and teammate Roger Maris' assault on the single-season home run record held by Babe Ruth. Crystal said he "wanted to make this movie since the first time I came to Yankee Stadium in 1956. Mickey Mantle hit a home run off the facade, and I've had a love affair with the Yankees and baseball ever since." Crystal also had a strong personal connection to the story, having become a close friend of his childhood hero Mantle in the mid-1970s, a relationship that lasted until Mantle's death in 1995. "Mickey once said to me, 'If they ever do a story about my life, I want you to be involved.' "

Billy Crystal (center) is joined by (from left) David and Danny Mantle, sons of Mickey Mantle, and Susan and Kevin Maris, daughter and son of Roger Maris, at the screening of 61* at Paramount Studios in Los Angeles in 2001.

Kevin Winter/Getty Images.

The concept of the daily press conference didn't exist in 1961, so writers descended on Mantle and Maris, surrounding them at their lockers for hours after the game. While Maris struggled with the constant media attention, it was no big deal to Mickey, who'd been handling the media crush since his rookie season in 1951. Over the course of a decade, Mickey had built a relationship with New York's baseball writers, so he willingly answered just about any question they posed. Misunderstood by the media, Maris offered this explanation: "I'm not trying to be Babe Ruth; I'm trying to hit 61 home runs and be Roger Maris."

C&G Collections/Getty Images

In mid-season, as Mantle and Maris launched home runs at an unheard-of rate, Commissioner Ford Frick intoned that unless the Ruth mark of 60 homers was bested in 154 or fewer games (the American League had expanded that year and increased the schedule to 162 games) they would be listed as separate records. The acerbic sportswriter Dick Young is widely credited with spreading the urban legend of the asterisk, which was never actually applied.

But much as it would be for Henry Aaron more than a decade later, the process of challenging a cherished Ruth record was harrowing. In Maris' case, it was even more difficult because he outpaced Mantle in the chase, with The Mick bowing out in the final weeks of the season with an injury.

Mantle's defense of his friend would remain a central theme in the decade that Mickey survived past Maris. "As far as I'm concerned, that's probably the greatest achievement in professional sports that I've ever seen," Mantle said in 1991. "Who was it that said there should be an asterisk? Ford Frick? They don't have it now and they never should have had it."

On the first day of spring training in 1961, new manager Ralph Houk made it clear that it would be Mickey Mantle's task to lead the charge on the field, just as he had done the past decade. Mantle, Ford, and Berra, who provided a link from the DiMaggio era, would make or break the Yankees during the transition from Casey Stengel to Houk.

In one of his first moves, Houk shifted Berra, now 36, to left field, finally getting Elston Howard in the lineup at catcher. Because he'd been an outfielder at the beginning of his career, Berra was willing to switch. Another change: Whitey Ford would pitch every fourth day. Previously, Stengel started Ford at most every fifth day, or only against the league's top teams, mainly due to worries about Ford's slight stature (5-foot-9, 160 pounds).

Houk's final major move was to flip-flop Mantle, who hit third in the batting order the previous year, and Maris, who hit fourth. The idea was to keep opponents from pitching around Maris. The move didn't look so hot in April; Mantle was hitting .455 with five homers and 11 RBI after 10 games while Maris was 5 for 31 (.161). Six weeks into the season, the Yankees were stumbling along with a 16-14 record, five games behind first-place Detroit.

Maris, with just four homers through May 22, visited an eye doctor, figuring he might have vision problems. When his eyes

Movie Star Mantle

I never shook Mickey Mantle's hand and that remains one of my few regrets. When I was 8 years old, Mickey stood right in front of me at the 86th Street RKO theatre. It was April 1962, and that silly movie *Safe at Home* had just come out to capitalize on The M&M Boy's 1961 season-long home run derby. The Yankee team made appearances in several New York City movie houses to promote the film.

I forced Dad to get to the theatre two hours early to make sure we were on the aisle. First, we had a quick burger across the street at Prexy's. At 7:05, word spread that the team bus had pulled up in front. The Yankees came into the lobby dressed in suits and ties and marched down the right side of the movie house. Yogi Berra walked by me and stepped on my toe, but I didn't notice, though my father did. He wanted Berra to apologize. (It was strange seeing Dad get mad at Yogi Berra.)

Elston Howard stopped in front of me and put his arms behind his back like a military MP. Ellie saw I was shaking in my sneakers over the sight of Mickey Mantle standing right next to him, two feet away from me. Dad and Ellie exchanged laughs over my dilemma, then Howard leaned over and whispered in my ear, "Say hi; he won't bite you." But I was too scared to say anything to Mickey. As the Yankees walked on stage for a final bow, I dribbled my opportunity away.

Then there was Mickey's 500th home run — Sunday, May 14, 1967. We cried while we hugged over that one; I miss Dad hugging me. I made him take me to the Friday, Saturday, and Sunday games that weekend. Friday night, Hal Reniff gave up nine runs in two innings of relief (Whitey Ford started), and the Yankees got pounded, but we stayed to watch Mick hit.

— Thomas R. Pryor, New York, New York

[Ed. note: In that three-game series against the Orioles, Baltimore beat the Yankees by 14-0 and 5-3 scores on Friday and Saturday. Mantle went 1 for 7, combined, in the first two games, but in the third, he was 2 for 4 with two runs, an RBI, and that 500th career homer. Fittingly, the Yankees won, 6-5.]

Little could pitcher Tracy Stallard imagine that he would be part of baseball history when he started his first full season with the Boston Red Sox in 1961. Yet there he was on the mound October 1 in the final game of the season facing Roger Maris and baseball immortality. Maris hit his 61st home run off a Stallard fastball in the fourth inning. Maris' achievement endures while Stallard became a footnote in baseball's timeless story. Even so, Stallard took pride in his role in the historic event. "I'm glad he did it off me," Stallard said later. "Otherwise, I would never have been thought of again." Stallard finished his career with a 30-57 record over seven seasons. This photograph capturing the monumental home run is signed by both Maris and Stallard. It sold at auction for $1,000.

Heritage Auction Galleries

blurred after he was given eye drops, Maris had to leave that night's game in the first inning. The same night, the Yankees started a 17-game stretch in which they bashed 32 homers, including seven in one game at Boston on Memorial Day. Mantle and Maris had two homers each in that game. The pair ended May with 26 homers between them: Mantle 14, Maris 12.

In June, the Yankees went 22-10, but the hot topic was Mantle vs. Maris vs. Babe Ruth. All summer long, the "M&M Boys" piled up the numbers; by August, Maris was atop the AL with 40 homers, and Mickey was on his heels with 39. Newspapers across the country started conducting polls, asking fans whether they wanted to see the record broken, and if so, by whom: Mantle or Maris?

There was little question about which slugger was more popular. Mantle, whose rags-to-riches story epitomized what America was all about, had been around for years and had won four home run titles. Maris, relatively unknown, wasn't particularly popular with sportswriters because he wasn't glib or outgoing. He was downright shy around strangers, particularly writers.

Naturally, stories started appearing about friction between Maris and Mantle, fueled by the supposed rivalry between the two as they pursued the most prestigious record in baseball. Nothing was further from the truth. Mantle and Maris had become fast friends; they were very much alike—incredible athletes and shy around strangers, but outgoing around people they trusted.

What few knew was that in 1961, Mantle, Maris, and backup outfielder Bob Cerv shared a New York apartment as a haven to escape from the madness that Yankee Stadium had become. The outfielders used to joke about the ludicrous stories detailing the feud between Maris and Mantle. They would shout, "Didja hear? I hate your guts." Then they'd laugh at the insanity of it all.

The race was made even more fascinating by circumstances set into motion years before. Since 1961 was the first year of American League expansion and the schedule increased from 154 to 162 games, several sportswriters asked the question: If someone had extra games to break the record, was it fair? The final decision was left to Commissioner Ford Frick, hardly an impartial observer. Before serving as National League president and then commissioner, Frick was a New York sportswriter who became Babe Ruth's confidant and the ghostwriter of his biography.

A Dream Meeting

People often ask me why I'm a Yankees fan and I always reply, "I grew up watching Mickey Mantle hit home runs in the World Series."

I saw him play three or four times in person—all at Anaheim Stadium in the mid-1960s—and one time I ventured down the aisle to the dugout and stood not three feet away from The Mick and Roger Maris. (Maris was in his T-shirt and had a pack of Winstons rolled up in his sleeve.) I remember being so awestruck that I couldn't say anything. It was like a dream.

One game Mickey had three singles and I told my brother Bill that I felt cheated (not really!). I told Bill I'd rather see Mickey strike out than hit a single.

I've read a lot about Mickey Mantle over the years. Jim Bouton's Ball Four, to me, greatly enhanced his legend. But the one thing that I'll always remember was the one time he said, "I was tryin' to hit a home run every time I swung the bat."

— John M. Sweeney, Anchorage, Alaska

First Impressions

In 1961, at the first baseball game I ever attended, I saw Mickey Mantle at Yankee Stadium make a diving catch and then double up a runner on first. The next inning he hit a shot that was a line drive over the right-field wall. I was 8 years old at the time, and I thought that I had just seen God.

— Michael Yonchenko, Kenwood, California

In the privacy of the locker room, Mantle and Maris relax and wash away the pressure of the home run chase with a cold beverage. This framed photo includes the autographs of both Mantle and Maris.

Heritage Auction Galleries

MANTLE BLASTS
565 FT. HOME RUN

Frick ruled that Ruth's record would stand unless Maris or Mantle broke it by the season's 154th game. The final eight games, Frick said, would give an unfair advantage to anyone chasing Ruth's record. "Asterisk" became the new catchword for the nation's baseball fans.

The home run race was one of the biggest stories to ever hit baseball. The concept of the daily press conference didn't exist at the time, so writers descended on Mantle and Maris, surrounding them at their lockers for hours after the game. It was no big deal to Mickey, who'd been handling the media crush since his rookie season in 1951. Over the course of a decade, Mickey had built a relationship with New York's baseball writers, so he willingly answered just about any question they posed.

Maris had no such experience with the media blitz. He'd played for the Cleveland Indians and Kansas City Athletics, hardly known for intense media coverage. Maris grew tired of repeatedly answering the same questions; finally, he would snap, make some sort of semi-sarcastic comment, and escape to the relative sanity of the showers.

The writers, in turn, described Maris as moody, uncooperative, and unpopular. They were right; he was all that—to sportswriters. But he was popular with his teammates because of his hustle and willingness to do whatever it took to win.

By the end of August, Maris had 51 homers, Mantle 48. All eyes were on the sluggers as they raced toward Babe's 60. By the way, there was a heated pennant race going on, too.

During Labor Day weekend, the red-hot Tigers, only 1 1/2 games behind the Yankees, came to the Bronx for a crucial series. Detroit, having won 11 of its last 14, featured sluggers Al Kaline, Norm Cash, and Rocky Colavito. The first game was a pitchers' duel. Detroit's Don Mossi shut down the Yankees, as Whitey Ford was doing until the fifth inning, when he pulled a leg muscle. Relievers Bud Daley and Luis Arroyo kept the Tigers at bay through nine innings, with some defensive help from Berra. After Bill Bruton walked with one out in the 8th inning, Kaline hit a line drive off the left-field wall. Berra played it perfectly and threw to second to nail a surprised Kaline. In the bottom of the 9th, the Yankees finally got to Mossi. Singles by Elston Howard, Berra, and Moose Skowron brought home the game's only run.

In the second game, Maris homered off Frank Lary and Hank Aguirre, giving him 53 home runs, as the Yankees topped Detroit, 5-2. Mantle, however, pulled a muscle in his left forearm trying to check a swing and

The Security Guard's Helper

MEMORIES OF MANTLE

My uncle was a cameraman at WPIX, the independent television station in New York that carried Yankee games. I went to the Stadium often and saw some memorable Mickey Mantle homers and great games, including the final game of 1961, when Roger Maris hit his 61st homer, and the opener of the 1963 World Series, when Sandy Koufax was invincible.

But my favorite Mantle memory was at a game when a couple of fans were really giving the business to Jimmy Piersall, who was in the outfield that day for one of his many employers [Piersall played for five different teams in his career]. One of the hecklers was idiotic enough to run onto the field, and Mantle appeared from nowhere to help corral the guy and kick him in the butt.

— Paul White, Phoenix, Arizona

left the game early. Writers, figuring Mantle would miss at least a week with the muscle pull, counted him out of the home run race.

Mantle had other ideas. He told Houk he could play and then proved it. In the third game of the Tigers series, he staked the Yankees to a 2-1 lead with a 400-foot rocket into the right field bleachers. His forearm was so sore he had to ice it between innings, but he didn't let it stop him.

The Tigers went ahead in the top of the 9th, 5-4, but Mantle tied the game in the bottom of the inning with another 400-foot homer to right field. Later that inning, Howard hit a three-run homer to give New York an 8-5 win. The Yankees' sweep over the Tigers, for all intents and purposes, sewed up their second straight American League pennant.

On the morning of September 4, the tally stood at 53 homers for Maris and 50 for Mantle, with the Washington Senators arriving for four games in three days. Mantle and Maris both homered in the series, a sweep for the Yankees.

Cleveland came to town next for a five-game series. In the first inning of the first game, Tony Kubek ripped a triple. When Maris brought him home with a bunt single, the writers went nuts. Why was Roger bunting when he was chasing Ruth's record? The answer: he wanted to win. Of course, in his next at bat, he hit homer number 55.

By September 10, the Yankees had swept the Indians and Maris had 56 homers, with Mantle three behind at 53. More important, the Yankees had a 12-game winning streak and an 11½-game lead over Detroit.

Mantle, though, was fighting a bad flu. Yankees broadcaster Mel Allen told him he knew a doctor who specialized in vitamin shots, which would fix Mickey up good as new. He took his referral and went to see Dr. Max Jacobson, who administered what became known as "The Shot."

Jacobson, who had reportedly treated stars such as Eddie Fisher, Elizabeth Taylor, and Tennessee Williams, stuck the needle into Mantle's hip higher than normal and grazed his hipbone. It put Mantle in such pain that he nearly passed out walking back to the St. Moritz Hotel. Merlyn Mantle was coming in from Dallas the next morning, but Mantle, running a high fever, couldn't get out of bed. He called the hotel manager to have someone pick up his wife at Union Station, and then he promptly passed out. Merlyn found him still in bed, sick and sweating, running a 104-degree temperature. She took him to Lenox Hill Hospital, where doctors lanced the wound to drain an infection that had set in overnight. Doctors said the bone was bruised; Mickey would be incapacitated for a while, basically ending his run at Ruth's record.

Mantle hit one more homer in the final three weeks of the season, but "The Shot" basically ended his 1961 season. He still led the league in three categories, attaining a .687 slugging percentage, tying Maris with 132 runs scored, and drawing a major-league-high 126 walks. Despite his injury troubles at the season's end, amazingly, he missed only nine games and finished at .317 with 54 homers and 128 RBIs.

On Sept. 20, in the 154th game of the season, Maris hit his 59th homer, blasting a fastball off Orioles starter Milt Pappas at Baltimore's Memorial Stadium. Twelve games later, in the season finale, Maris hit No. 61 off Boston's Tracy Stallard.

Mantle, unfortunately, wasn't at Yankee Stadium on the big day. He was in the hospital, battling the virus that originally drove him to Dr. Jacobson. He was, however, in uniform for the World Series, though he played in only two of the five games against the Cincinnati Reds. He literally had a hole in his leg—an oozing sore packed with gauze to soak up blood and pus from the infection. The sight of the wound made Skowron and Kubek so nauseous they had to leave the trainer's room while team doctor Sidney Gaynor removed the packing from the wound.

Mantle sat out the first two games of the World Series, but in batting practice before Game 3 at Crosley Field in Cincinnati, he hit six balls into the stands in 10 swings. Houk took note and gave Mickey the start in center the next night, much to the delight of Yankees fans. Alas, Mick didn't do much, going 0 for 4 and handling few chances in the field (Berra and Maris took everything they could to alleviate the pressure on Mantle's leg).

Mantle did, however, inspire the Yankees, who won the third game, 3-2, aided by a Maris homer in the top of the 9th inning. In Game 4, Mantle singled off Jim O'Toole in the 4th inning, but then he made a big mistake: he tried to break up a double play. His slide into second base ripped open the sore on his leg, forcing him to leave the game.

Mantle tried to convince Houk to leave him in the game, but enough was enough; his uniform pants were soaked with blood from his waist to his knee. Just like that, Mantle was through for the season. The Yankees, though, reclaimed the world championship, beating the Reds in five games to cap an unprecedented season.

1961

Regular Season

Year	Age	G	AB	R	H	2B	3B	HR	RBI	SB	BB	SO	BA
1961	29	153	514	132	163	16	6	54	128	12	126	112	.317

World Series

Year	Age	G	AB	R	H	2B	3B	HR	RBI	SB	BB	SO	BA
1961	29	2	6	0	1	0	0	0	0	0	0	2	.167

Noteworthy

· Mantle battles Roger Maris throughout the summer in pursuit of Babe Ruth's single-season HR record.
· In addition to finishing second to Maris in HRs, Mantle leads the AL in walks and slugging percentage (.687).
· Mantle's regular season ends early when he enters the hospital on Sept. 29 with a hip infection, though he does return to play in two World Series games.
· The Yankees, after posting a 109-53 regular-season record, beat the Reds in five games in the World Series.

Mantle and Maris enjoy a quiet moment in the locker room after Maris hit his 59th home run of the season against Baltimore September 20.

Herb Scharfman/Sports Imagery/Getty Images

Clare Ruth, the widow of Babe Ruth, graciously accepts a kiss from Roger Maris after he hit his 60th home run of the season to tie Babe Ruth's single-season record September 26, 1961. Together, the two hold the ball Maris hit during the third inning against Baltimore's Jack Fisher at Yankee Stadium. This AP wire photo includes the printed caption, noting Commissioner Ford Frick's ruling that would attach the asterisk to the Yankee slugger's accomplishment. The asterisk Fricke championed never appeared in record books. The photo was signed by Maris years after the home run and sold at auction for $1,135.25.

Heritage Auction Galleries

(NY51) NEW YORK, Sept. 26--MARIS MEETS WIDOW OF CHAMPION--Roger Maris kisses Mrs. Clare Ruth on meeting after game tonight at New York's Yankee Stadium. Between them they hold ball Maris hit during third inning of game against Baltimore for his 60th homerun of season. Mrs. Ruth, widow of Babe Ruth who holds record with 60 homeruns, congratulated the Yankee outfielder. Maris is second man in major league history to collect 60 homeruns in one season. By ruling of Ford Frick, based on extended season, Maris does not officially tie Ruth's record. (AP Wirephoto)(rwt32332stf)61 (See AP Sports Wire Story)

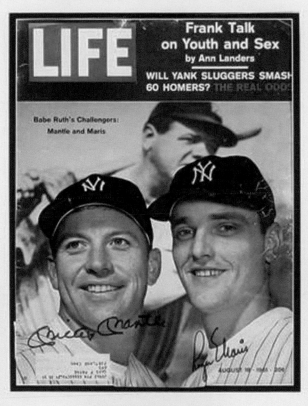

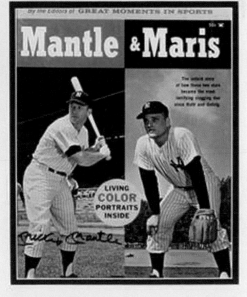

This amazing collage celebrating the most exciting pinstriped duo since Lou Gehrig and Babe Ruth is anchored by a 1961 Life magazine at center, which begs the question "Will Yank Sluggers Smash 60 Homers?" Both Mantle and Maris signed the Life cover. To the right the pair appears again, on an 8 x 10-inch black and white photo. Mantle also signed solo a 1960s magazine picturing the pair. Six unsigned images of the historic pair fill out the rest of the display area. Matted and framed, the piece is 33 x 34 inches. It sold for $2,868 at auction.

Heritage Auction Galleries

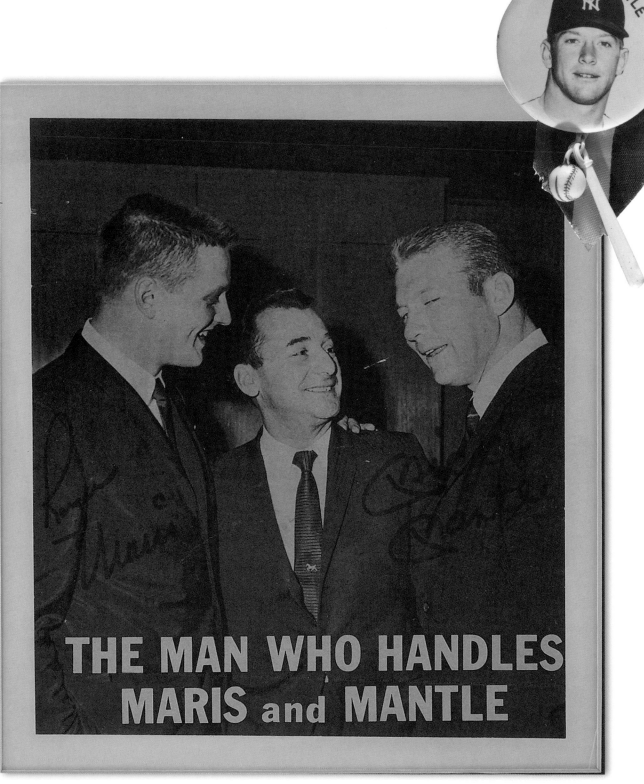

THE MAN WHO HANDLES MARIS and MANTLE

Vintage Roger Maris and Mickey Mantle stadium-issued pinbacks with ribbons and charms.

Heritage Auction Galleries

Imagine representing both Mickey Mantle and Roger Maris at the height of their celebrity. Such was the luck of their agent Frank Scott. A former Yankee official, Scott was baseball's first player agent. Besides Maris and Mantle, Scott's clients included Joe DiMaggio, Willie Mays, Henry Aaron, Whitey Ford, Duke Snider, Gil Hodges, Larry Doby, Walter Alston, Ralph Branca, Bob Feller, and Roy Campanella. He also represented Vince Lombardi, Frank Gifford and Y. A. Tittle from football and Oscar Robertson and Bob Cousy from basketball. Autographed by both Mantle and Maris, this image sold for $1,553 at auction.

Heritage Auction Galleries

NEW YORK YANKEES
1961 WORLD CHAMPIONS

First Row, Left to Right: WHITEY FORD, BILL SKOWRON, HAL RENIFF, JIM HEGAN, FRANK CROSETTI, RALPH HOUK, JOHN SAIN, WALLY MOSES, EARL TORGESON, CLETIS BOYER, YOGI BERRA, MICKEY MANTLE.

Second Row, Left to Right: GUS MAUCH (TRAINER), BILLY GARDNER, BOB HALE, JOE DE MAESTRI, TONY KUBEK, TEX CLEVENGER, RALPH TERRY, HECTOR LOPEZ, BOB CERV, ELSTON HOWARD, ROGER MARIS, BOB TURLEY, JOE SOARES (TRAINER).

Third Row, Left to Right: BOBBY RICHARDSON, AL DOWNING, LUIS ARROYO, JOHN BLANCHARD, BILL STAFFORD, ROLAND SHELDON, JIM COATES, SPUD MURRAY (BATTING PRACTICE PITCHER), BUD DALEY, BRUCE HENRY (TRAVELING SECRETARY).

Seated on Ground in Front: Batboys FRANK PRUDENTI, FRED BENGIS.

This 1961 New York Yankees team picture was autographed by Roger Maris. The team included, front row (from left) batboys Frank Prudenti and Fred Bengis. Second row: Whitey Ford, Bill Skowron, Hal Reniff, Jim Hegan, Frank Crosetti, Ralph Houk, John Sain, Wally Moses, Earl Torgeson, Clete Boyer, Yogi Berra, and Mickey Mantle. Third row: Gus Mauch (trainer), Billy Gardner, Bob Hale, Joe DeMaestri, Tony Kubek, Tex Clevenger, Ralph Terry, Hector Lopez, Bob Cerv, Elston Howard, Roger Maris, Bob Turley, and Joe Soares (trainer). Fourth row: Bobby Richardson, Al Downing, Luis Arroyo, Johnny Blanchard, Bill Stafford, Roland Sheldon, Jim Coates, Spud Murray (batting practice pitcher), Bud Daley, and Bruce Henry (traveling secretary).

Heritage Auction Galleries

As illustrated by this *Life* magazine cover, Babe Ruth cast an imposing shadow over one of the most memorable seasons in baseball history.

Heritage Auction Galleries

FACING:

Mantle shared the Yankee Stadium spotlight with Roger Maris in 1961 during one of the greatest home run races in baseball history.

© Ozzie Sweet

A signed Roger Maris baseball.

October 1, 1961, began a new era in baseball. This is the day Roger Maris eclipsed the long-standing record of Babe Ruth to become the new single-season home run king. This program, ticket stub, and rain check are from that day. The program cover has been written on in ink and an excited fan even illustrated where Maris' 61st home run landed. This historically significant set sold for $1,500 at auction.

Heritage Auction Galleries

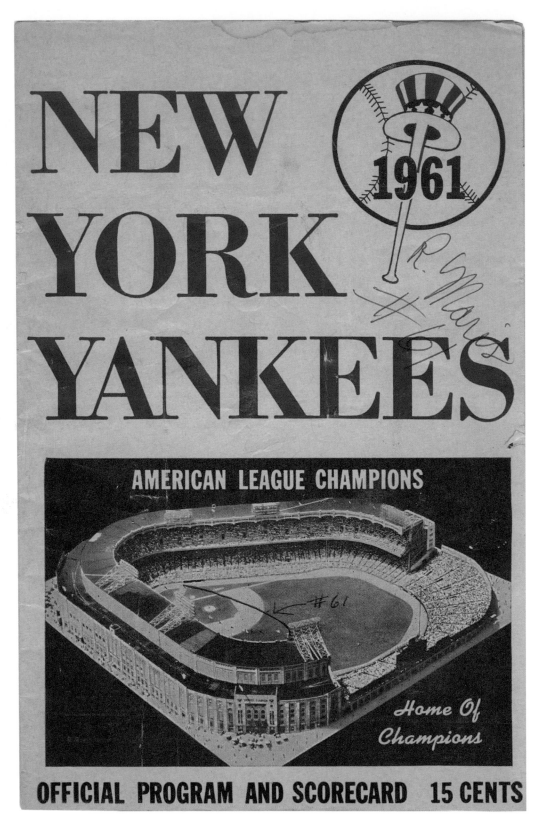

The 1961 season has gone down as one of the greatest in baseball history. The season, however, was about more than home runs. It was a testament to teammates and personal perseverance that stands today as a monument to two great players: Roger Maris and Mickey Mantle.

Heritage Auction Galleries

Two of baseball's greatest sluggers, Mantle and St. Louis Cardinal all-time great Stan "The Man" Musial, pose for newspaper photographers prior to a game.

Heritage Auction Galleries

The baseball that Mantle struck for home run No. 16 in the 1964 World Series sold for $80,000 at auction.

Drysdale, Johnny Podres, and Ron Perranoski limited the Yankees to only four runs, 22 base hits, and a .171 average in the four-game sweep. Mantle's average was even worse than the team's; he batted an anemic .133 (2 for 15), with one home run.

After the Series, Houk resigned as manager to become the team's general manager. In a move that surprised almost everyone in with baseball, Houk named Yogi Berra as the new Yankees manager.

Despite Yogi's knowledge of the game, some of the younger players were prone to ignoring him. His old friend Mickey Mantle may have had a hand in their belligerence, albeit unintentionally. At Yogi's first clubhouse meeting in the spring of 1964, he laid out rules he expected his players to follow. When he finished, Mantle got up from his chair, threw his arms in the air, and yelled "I quit!"—and then stormed out of the room in fake anger. His teammates, according to reports, were in hysterics, and even Yogi smiled, but it may have set the tone for the season.

The Yankees got off to a slow start, falling six games behind the White Sox by June 10. They rallied to win 13 of their next 15 games, taking over first place for a day before faltering again. All summer long they jockeyed for position with the White Sox and Orioles. Mantle's hitting helped to keep the Yankees close. There was his two-homer, three-RBI game in a win at Boston on June 11, for example. There was his three-hit, two RBI game in a win over the White Sox two days later. And there was his three-run, 8th-inning homer to beat the Twins on the 4th of July.

Still, the Yankees struggled to break away from the pack. By August 20, they seemed to be sinking fast. They were in the midst of a six-game losing streak, having been shut out that night on a seven-hitter by John Buzhardt in Chicago. And they found themselves 4½ games behind the White Sox and 4 games behind Baltimore.

After that loss to Chicago, as the Yankees' team bus snaked its way through traffic, infielder Phil Linz sat in the back playing a dirge-like version of "Mary Had a Little Lamb" on a harmonica; he had just bought it and was learning to play. The noise bugged Berra, who was fuming in the front seat, so he told Linz to put away the harmonica. Linz didn't hear what Berra said, so Mantle turned around and relayed an errant message: "He said to play it louder." So Linz carried on, prompting Berra to storm to the back of the bus and slap the harmonica out of his hands.

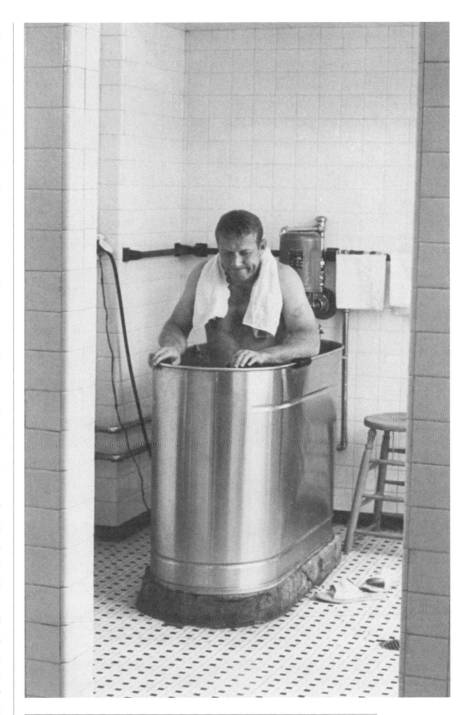

The rigors of playing ball on bum knees finally caught up with Mantle. The pain, somewhat relieved by soaking in a whirlpool in the clubhouse after a game, robbed Mantle of his speed and, eventually, his career.

John Dominis//Time Life Pictures/Getty Images

Not surprisingly, 1962 was a busy year for Mickey Mantle and Roger Maris. Following their epic home run race, Mantle and Maris were in high demand. After completing the filming of Safe at Home in March, another film offer was waiting in the wings. This time Mantle, Maris, and Yogi Berra worked with two of Hollywood's biggest stars, Cary Grant and Doris Day, in That Touch of Mink. Even though their camera time was relatively short, it was noteworthy. The scene, which was filmed inside the Yankees dugout, showed the ballplayers all being ejected from the game by umpire Art Passarella. Directed by Delbert Mann, the movie was released on June 14, 1962, and also featured Gig Young, Audrey Meadows, John Astin, and Laurie Mitchell.

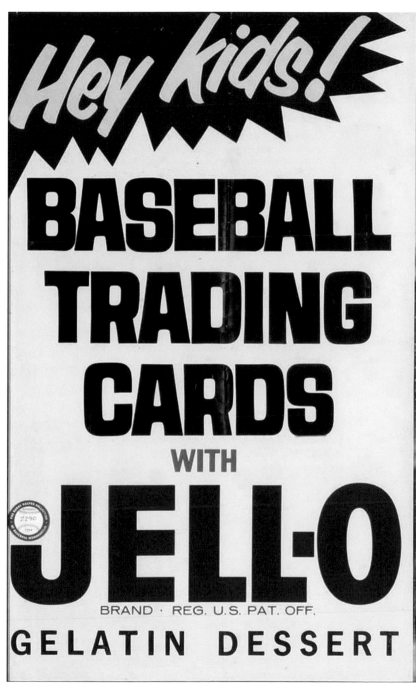

Tremendously rare and desirable, this 1962-63 Jell-O advertising poster measures 30 x 35 inches. Mantle signed the piece, adding the Jell-O slogan "um, um Good." It sold for nearly $7,200 at auction.

Heritage Auction Galleries

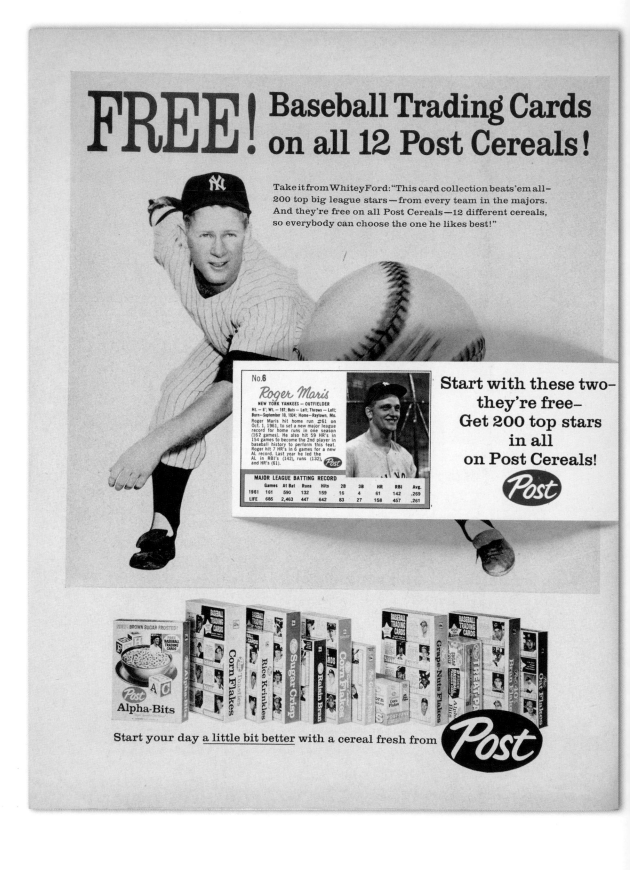

Mickey Mantle and Roger Maris were part of the Post Cereal baseball cards offered inside the April 13, 1962, issue of *Life* magazine. The complete 200-card set featured such stars as Yogi Berra, Whitey Ford, Al Kaline, Carl Yastrzemski, Sandy Koufax, Willie Mays, Henry Aaron, and Roberto Clemente, among a host of others.

Heritage Auction Galleries

CHAPTER FOUR

No.5
Mickey Mantle
NEW YORK YANKEES — OUTFIELDER
Ht—6'; Wt—200; Switch Hitter; Throws—Right;
Born—October 20, 1931; Home—Dallas, Texas
The AL's home-run king for the 4th
time in 1960 (40), he also finished 2nd
for the MVP Award. Mickey won the MVP
title in 1956, with a BA of .353, and
again in 1957 with a BA of .365 (his all-
time high). He has hit 14 World Series
HR's—one behind Ruth's record of 15.
He ranks 6th in lifetime HR's with
374. All-Star Games (1953-1961).

MAJOR LEAGUE BATTING RECORD

	Games	At Bat	Runs	Hits	2B	3B	HR	RBI	Avg.
1961	153	514	131	163	16	6	54	128	.317
LIFE	1,552	5,519	1,244	1,700	241	66	374	1,063	.308

**Start with these two—
they're free—
Get 200 top stars
in all
on Post Cereals!**

Post

Sunbeam Frypan doubles as Mother Hen

We're not in the business of raising chickens, but we did try it in a Sunbeam frypan to make a rather important point.

To hatch chicks, a mother hen has to keep the eggs at a carefully controlled even heat of 101 degrees Fahrenheit.

That's why a Sunbeam automatic frypan could handle the job. It's precision made (in the Sunbeam tradition) to keep the heat under things you cook at a constant tempera-ture, depending on where you set the dial. This takes the "guess" out of cooking—gives you meals you can be proud of every time.

The extra high dome cover takes even a nine pound roast, and buffet style handles make for gracious serving.

Treat yourself to a new Sunbeam buffet style Multi-Cooker frypan. You'll be proud as a mother hen.

Sunbeam CORPORATION
The best electric appliances made
CHICAGO 50, ILLINOIS   TORONTO 18, CANADA
© S.C. ® SUNBEAM

MEMORIES OF MANTLE

Now Batting ...

I think my strongest memory of Mickey Mantle is how even the announcement of his name, or his appearance in the on-deck circle, would cause fans to cheer—even after 1964, when there wasn't much to cheer about. He was a living link to Ruth, Gehrig, DiMaggio, and the rest. It's difficult to convey today how much he meant to people growing up in that era.

— Michael A. Livingston,
Cheltenham, Pennsylvania

ROGER MARIS, WILLIE MAYS, MICKEY MANTLE

The 1962 World Series featured two of the finest center fielders in baseball history: Willie Mays and Mickey Mantle. Spicing up the series was the presence of Roger Maris, who the year before electrified the country while surpassing Babe Ruth's single-season home run record. Although the Yankees won the series in seven games, there was no mistaking the greatness of Mays. In 1969, after Mays hit his 600th home run, *The Sporting News* honored him as its player of the decade; in later years it named him the second-greatest player of all time, right behind Babe Ruth.

Heritage Auction Galleries

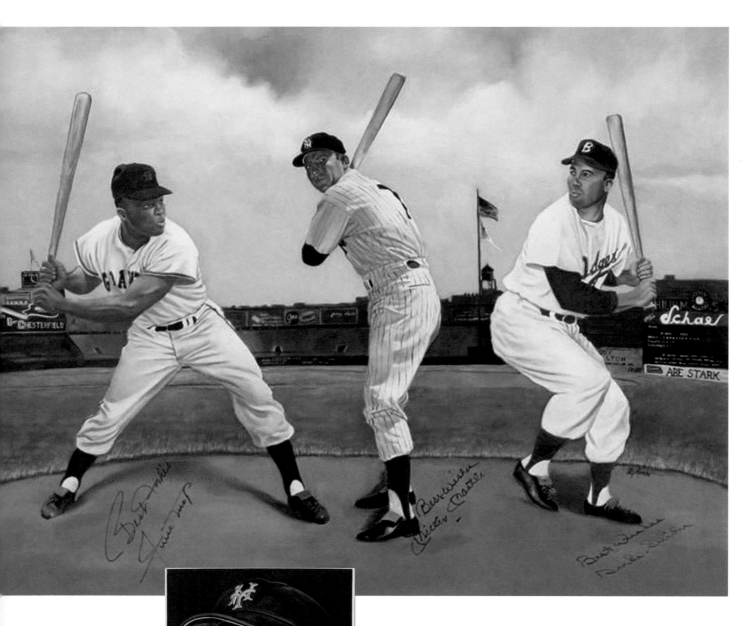

In the oil painting at left, sports artist Flip Amato depicted Willie Mays, Mickey Mantle, and Duke Snider in the vastness of the old Polo Grounds. The 23 x 30-inch painting was signed by each player in blue Sharpie. The painting sold for $1,300 at auction.

Heritage Auction Galleries

This autographed Willie Mays portrait by famed sports artist Andy Jurinko sold for nearly $2,000 at auction. Jurinko is widely recognized as one of the nation's premier sports artists, joining Leroy Neiman and Robert Simon as the hobby's most collectible painters. Jurinko grew up a baseball fan in Philadelphia. Having completed more than 600 baseball-themed pieces, Jurinko's work has been featured in such publications as *The New York Times*, *Sports Illustrated*, and *New York Magazine*, and is part of the permanent collection of The Baseball Hall of Fame.

Heritage Auction Galleries

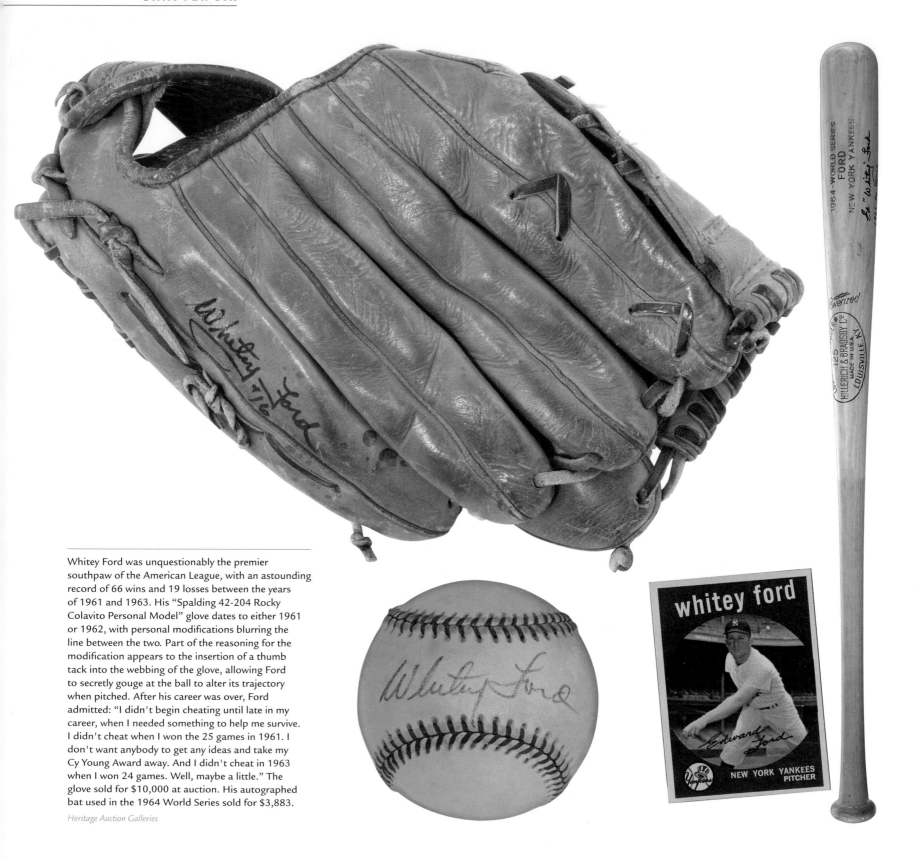

Whitey Ford was unquestionably the premier southpaw of the American League, with an astounding record of 66 wins and 19 losses between the years of 1961 and 1963. His "Spalding 42-204 Rocky Colavito Personal Model" glove dates to either 1961 or 1962, with personal modifications blurring the line between the two. Part of the reasoning for the modification appears to the insertion of a thumb tack into the webbing of the glove, allowing Ford to secretly gouge at the ball to alter its trajectory when pitched. After his career was over, Ford admitted: "I didn't begin cheating until late in my career, when I needed something to help me survive. I didn't cheat when I won the 25 games in 1961. I don't want anybody to get any ideas and take my Cy Young Award away. And I didn't cheat in 1963 when I won 24 games. Well, maybe a little." The glove sold for $10,000 at auction. His autographed bat used in the 1964 World Series sold for $3,883.

Heritage Auction Galleries

So Close...

I remember looking at a *Daily News* story about Mickey Mantle hitting the facade at the old Yankee Stadium [May 22, 1963] and being dumbstruck at the diagram showing the flight of the ball, and how it would have cleared the roof if it had been hit a bit higher or if the angle was different.

I'm 63 and grew up a Yankees fan. I still get a great feeling remembering Mickey Mantle and the Yankees of my youth. Baseball then seemed so much more real.

—Nickey Newark, New York, New York

They called Whitey Ford "The Chairman of the Board" for good reason. He was for more than a decade the star pitcher of a team that operated with corporate efficiency. The Yankees won 11 pennants in Ford's years with them. He ranks first all-time in World Series wins (10), games and games started (22), innings pitched, hits, bases on balls, and strikeouts. In the 1960, 1961 and 1962 Series, he pitched 33 and 2/3 consecutive scoreless innings, breaking Babe Ruth's record of 29 and 2/3. A fun-loving native New Yorker, Whitey formed a curious odd couple with Oklahoman Mickey Mantle. The two were inducted into the Hall of Fame together in 1974. This unframed 16" x 20" photo of Ford in pitching motion has been signed in bold blue Sharpie with HOF 74 inscription added.

Heritage Auction Galleries

1965-1968: The Final Years

BY THE END OF THE 1964 SEASON, Mickey Mantle's body was in rough shape. Around that time, fans could read in newspapers and magazines a laundry list of his injuries and surgeries over the years:

1947: osteomyelitis

1951: cartilage operation on right knee

1952: second cartilage operation on right knee

1953: torn left thigh muscle and buckled right knee (ligaments)

1954: cyst removal operation behind right knee

1955: severely pulled right thigh muscle

1956: sprained left knee and tonsillectomy

1957: torn muscles in right shoulder

1959: fractured right index finger

1961: abscess requiring surgery

1962: severely pulled right thigh muscle and badly bruised left knee

1963: torn rib cage; broken metatarsal bone in left foot; damaged cartilage in left knee

FACING:
In a touching show of respect, Senator Robert F. Kennedy shakes Mantle's hand during "Mickey Mantle Day" at Yankee Stadium, September 18, 1965. Uncertain of his future, the Yankees chose to honor Mantle before he played in his 2,000th game with the team. Among the gifts Mantle receives during the ceremonies are two quarter horses.

RIGHT:
A 1966 Mantle game-worn road jersey sold for nearly $90,000 in 2009.

Heritage Auction Galleries

LIFE

MANTLE'S MISERY
He faces physical pain and a fading career

Mickey Mantle at 33,
in his 15th year with
the New York Yankees

JULY 30 · 1965 · 35¢

Obviously, opponents knew about Mantle's aches and pains. In the 1964 World Series, the Cardinals' scouting report noted that they could run on Mantle—and they did, taking extra bases that no team would have tried a few years prior.

Fans also understood that Mantle was playing in pain and they increasingly were showing appreciation, giving him ovations just for coming out of the dugout. It was a vast change from the booing he heard early in his career, when he was a young player who wasn't yet living up to his advance billing as a Ruth/Gehrig/DiMaggio combination.

In 1965, Mantle was 33 and headed into his twilight years as a player, and he found himself on a Yankee team that was trapped between rebuilding and defending its AL crown. Mantle also found himself with another new manager: Johnny Keane, a drill sergeant compared to the ousted Yogi Berra, and his style didn't play well with the team's veterans. Furthermore, Mantle found himself in left field; Keane decided to go with Tom Tresh and Roger Repoz, who started 103 and 58 games, respectively, in center.

Between the managerial and position changes, an assortment of injury flare-ups, and Mantle's own inconsistency, 1965 was a rough season for Mickey. His .255 average was his lowest up to that point; his production dipped, too, to 19 homers and 46 RBIs. He even considered retiring at various points during the season, with one of the low points coming in late June, when he missed 15 games and was relegated to pinch-hit duties in six others.

But like all great players, Mantle had his moments. On July 15, for example, in a Thursday night game at a hardly crowded Yankee Stadium (15,964 in attendance), Mantle homered in the 6th inning to tie a game the Yankees later won in 12 innings. On August 6 and 7, he hit homers on back-to-back nights, one right-handed, one left-handed. There was a grand slam against the Angels in California on September 2 and, two days later against Boston, another homer—the 473rd of his career.

Who knew whether Mantle would return in 1966, regardless of how close he was to entering the then-exclusive 500-home-run club? The Yankees had their doubts, so the team pulled together "Mickey Mantle Day" at Yankee Stadium on September 18. A Saturday afternoon crowd of 51,664 watched the Tigers spoil Mickey's day with a 4-3 win in 10 innings (Mantle was 0 for 3 with a walk). At least, though, Yankee fans had the chance to honor No. 7 and listen to a few words he delivered in a short speech after

Mickey's "Last Great Game"

I'm a lifelong Met fan but I always loved Mickey Mantle. I would sometimes go see the Yankees play, and one of my greatest memories ever is going to a Memorial Day doubleheader in 1968 [May 30] with a couple of friends. It was Mickey Mantle's last great game as a Yankee. In that first game, he went 5 for 5 with two homers and a double plus three runs and five runs batted in. It was like time had stood still—like it was 1961 again.

My last memory of the day is that Mantle did not play in the second game. He was ready to pinch-hit in the 9th inning with the Yankees losing, 6-2, and two outs. The last out was made with Mickey on one knee in the on-deck circle. As usual, he had to struggle to stand up, and then he walked slowly back to the dugout. That image was a stark reality to an otherwise all-time goose-bump day.

— Eric Friedman, Manalapan, New Jersey

being introduced. He thanked all those who helped him during his decade and a half with the Yankees, and closed with the line, "I just wish I had 15 more years with you."

By spring of 1966, Mantle felt refreshed enough to return to the Yankees, but he wasn't coming back to a replenished lineup. The team lost 16 of its first 20 games, and just like that, Keane found himself without a job.

Moving from the front office back into the dugout was Ralph Houk, a Mantle favorite. Houk got the Yankees playing a little closer to .500 ball the rest of the way, posting a 66-73 record (a .475 percentage). But fans weren't impressed. Attendance in 1966 was down, and it reached an embarrassing level on Thursday, September 22, when the smallest crowed in Stadium history (413 people) watched Joel Horlen and Hoyt Wilhelm of the White Sox beat the Yankees, 4-1. Mantle was out with an injury, but old standbys Roger Maris, Clete Boyer, and Tom Tresh played, as did rookie Bobby Murcer, who drove in the team's only run. Sadly, the Yankees fired longtime TV announcer Red Barber because he talked about the small crowed and directed cameramen to televise empty seats.

There's an old saying in sports: Father Time is undefeated. That means even the greatest players succumb to age and injuries. And so it was for Mantle, who, nearing the end of his glorious career, could no longer conjure up the magic of his youth.

Mark Kauffman//Time Life Pictures/Getty Images

For Mantle, 1966 was truly a season of ups and downs. He returned to center field and played errorless ball, but he also missed more than 50 games. Even in limited time, though, he hit 23 homers and batted .288.

And, of course, there were more moments of Mantle magic that gave fans lasting memories. On July 7, in the bottom of the 9th in a tie game against the Red Sox, Mantle hit a two-out, three-run walk-off homer off right-hander Don McMahon to give the Yankees a 5-2 win. Sixteen days later, Mantle sent the Yankee Stadium crowd into a frenzy with a 3rd-inning grand slam off the Angels' Marcelino Lopez, although the Yankees eventually lost the game.

On August 26, Mantle produced another walk-off homer. This one came off Tigers right-hander Hank Aguirre—a two-run blast to give the Yankees a 6-5 win. It was Mickey's 23rd and final homer of the season and 496th of his career. Mantle limped to the end of the season, missing all but five games in September. The year was equally forgettable for the Yankees. The team posted a 70-89 record, finishing a distant 26½ games behind the league-leading Baltimore Orioles. The Yankees finished last in the American League, the first time they had done that since 1912.

Ralph Houk returned as the Yankees' skipper in 1967 with a plan to move Mantle to first base in an effort to reduce the wear and tear on his legs. Even though it would keep Mick's bat in the lineup, the move to the infield actually caused concern that Mantle would get injured in a collision with a sprinting base runner. "I just hope I'm not the poor sucker who bowls him over," former teammate Moose Skowron, who played with the Angels in 1967, told a reporter. "It would be a terrible thing to have on your mind."

Despite the worries, the experiment worked. Mantle played in more games, 144, than he had since 1961. His batting average dropped to a career-low .245 but some of the dip was due to his leg injuries; he no longer beat out ground balls for infield hits as he had in the past.

Even so, Mantle was a force in the lineup. Pitchers continued working around him. Mantle was walked 107 times (only Harmon Killebrew drew more free passes among all major leaguers). And Mick did hit 22 more homers in 1967, the most memorable of which came on May 14 against the Orioles. Mantle blasted his 500th career home run off Stu Miller in the 3rd inning of a game at Yankee Stadium. Amazingly, the paid attendance that day was only 18,872.

The 1967 Yankees simply weren't capturing the imagination of fans. There wasn't a .300 hitter in the lineup, nor was there a long-ball threat other than Mantle (Pepitone hit just 13 and Tresh only 14). There wasn't much speed, either, other than Horace Clarke (21

MEMORIES OF MANTLE

A Grand Sight for a Kid

I idolized Mickey when I was a kid, even though I didn't become a fan of baseball until sometime around 1964-65, when Mickey Mantle started to decline.

My standout memory of Mantle is from a game I saw at Yankee Stadium between the Angels and the Yankees in 1966 [July 23]. Mantle came to the plate with the bases loaded and the Yankees down 3-0. My father turned to me and said that the pitcher would be better off just walking Mantle.

Sure enough, a couple of pitches later, Mantle hit the ball into the right field stands for a grand slam. Everyone — including me — went nuts. I had never, and have never since, heard such a deafening roar. The Yankees eventually lost the game 7-6, but I will always remember that home run.

—Robert Gall, Wheeling, West Virginia

MEMORIES OF MANTLE

Houston, We Have a Home Run

I was 18 in 1965 when the Yankees played an exhibition game in Houston. It was the first game ever at the brand new Houston Astrodome, and I remember Mickey Mantle hitting a home run off Turk Farrell. Mickey might have been nearing the end of his career, but I knew I was just plain lucky to be there.

— Bob Patterson, Austin, Texas

A Young Girl's First Hero

I've loved The Mick as long as I can remember. I think I fell deeply in love with him watching a post-game interview that followed a late-1950s game in which he was typically heroic. I don't remember exactly all that he had done in that game, but I believe it included two home runs.

Anyway, I remember him sitting kind of slouched on a wooden bench with a cement block wall behind him as the interviewer tried to get him to comment on his feats. Mantle deflected the attention from his own play by saying, dimples flashing, something like, "I'm just happy that we won; I'm glad for the team." It sounds trite today, but back then it came across to me, then a 7-year old, as heartfelt and real and truly modest.

I still have a large [bed]sheet that my sister and I and a friend of ours decorated and displayed as we marched on the field at Yankee Stadium on "Banner Day." The sheet reads "Mamaroneck, NY, loves the Mick." My sister inscribed the corner of the sheet with these words: "This splendid banner graced Yankee Stadium and was on television on May 10, 1968."

— Elizabeth Lang, New York, N.Y.

steals). Instead of names like Roger Maris (who had been traded to St. Louis), Clete Boyer (Braves), and Bobby Richardson (retired), the Yankees had Steve Whitaker, Charley Smith, and Ruben Amaro.

To make matters worse, Whitey Ford retired on May 30. "My fastball isn't as fast as it once was," he said before the season, "and my breaking stuff isn't as sharp." Yet he started out the season pitching as effectively as ever: Ford threw a 7-hit shutout at the White Sox on April 25, and allowed only eight earned runs in 44 innings (a 1.64 ERA) through mid-May. Unfortunately, an elbow injury ended his season and career.

With Ford gone, Mantle became the last link to the great 1950s-era Yankees. And on some afternoons and evenings in 1967, he'd do something special to remind fans of the glory days. Like on April 30, when he pulled a Minnie Rojas pitch into the right-field seats in the bottom of the 9th inning with two runners on base,

giving his team a thrilling 4-1 victory. Or on June 24, when he hit another game-winning walk-off homer, this time beating the Tigers and relief ace Fred Gladding, whose ERA that year was 1.99.

Overall, though, highlights were rare for the 1967 Yankees. In a particularly brutal one-month stretch starting on April 30, they went 6-16; as spring turned into summer and then fall, they struggled through two five-game losing streaks and two six-game losing streaks.

The team struggled as mightily as Mantle, finishing ahead of only the Kansas City Athletics in the American League final standings, with a record of 72-90, and a full 20 games behind the league-leading Boston Red Sox. Mantle himself managed only two hits in his final 31 at-bats, ending the season on a 0-for-15 slide.

Throughout the latter part of the 1967 season, American League teams had been bidding Mantle farewell, but surely he wouldn't close out his career with a slump like that... would he? To the delight of fans, Mickey returned in 1968 for one last season. His decision may have surprised some, especially those who knew how much pain he had endured throughout his career. Yankee trainer Joe Soares told writer Jim Ogle in early 1968, "Mickey has a greater capacity to withstand pain than any man I've ever seen. Some of the things he has done while in great pain are absolutely unbeliev-able. Believe me, some doctors have seen X-rays of his legs and won't believe they are the legs of an athlete still active."

Yet when the Yankees' training camp opened in 1968, Mantle was on hand for his 18th season. One of the team's unusual match-ups that spring involved a road trip to Mexico for a series of four exhibition games. The series drew 93,600 fans, a Mexico City re-cord for an international series at the time.

The Yankees lost to the Mexico City Reds in the first game of the series, and then beat the Mexico City Tigers in the second. Mantle gave the local fans a treat with a long home run in the third game, a 9-1 win over the Reds. In the finale, a Yankees win over the Tigers, Mantle found out how popular he had become when the Mexico City fans actually booed their own team for walking him in the first inning.

After returning home, the Yankees finished spring training and launched into the 1968 regular season. Everywhere the Yankees went fans gave Mantle standing ovations, fully appreciative of his abilities and his courage.

Despite constant pain in his knees near the end of his career, Mantle could still catch opponents off guard by dropping down a bunt and flashing some of his old speed for a base hit, as he showed here in a game in 1967. For his career, Mantle stole 153 bases while gettomg caught only 38 times.

Tony Tomsic/WireImage/Getty Images

Between the managerial and position changes and an assortment of injuries, 1965 was a rough season for Mantle. He played in 122 games and batted .255, the lowest of his career to that point. His power numbers also slumped. Mantle hit 19 home runs and drove in 46 runs; both the lowest of his career to that point when playing more than 100 games.

Of course, 1968 was the year of the pitcher—the year when Denny McLain won 31 games and Bob Gibson posted a 1.12 ERA. Only one American League hitter batted over .300: Carl Yastrzemski (and just barely, at .301).

Mantle wasn't immune to baseball's depressed batting averages. He batted only .237, dropping his career mark under .300 to .298. Throughout the rest of his life, he expressed regrets about that .002, saying on more than one occasion that he wished he hadn't played that last season.

Mantle's final season at least allowed him to push his career home run total past two members of the 500 Home Run Club: Ted Williams and Jimmie Foxx. Mantle passed Williams with his 522nd homer on May 6 off Sam McDowell. Moving ahead of Foxx was more of an ordeal. For four weeks, Mick was stuck on 534, the same number Foxx hit. And then he got an unexpected lift from an opponent. On September 19, McLain—on his way to a second straight Cy Young Award and a Tigers world championship—wanted to give Mantle a going-away present in his final at-bat in Detroit.

With the Tigers leading by a safe 6-1 margin in the 8th inning, McLain told catcher Jim Price to let Mantle know what was coming. Price did so, but Mickey didn't believe him. McLain went into his windup and then tossed a meatball down the middle. Mantle, incredulous, let it go. On the next pitch, Mantle didn't hesitate, slamming the ball into the upper deck at Tiger Stadium for home run No. 535.

Mantle was able to hit one more home run to finish two ahead of Foxx. The night after he hit No. 535, the Yanks were playing Boston on September 20. It was a close game, so Red Sox starter Jim Lonborg wasn't giving anything away. In the 3rd inning, with Boston up 1-0, Mantle connected with his final major-league home run. At the time, only two players in major league history had more: Babe Ruth and Willie Mays.

As he had done in 1967, Mantle ended the 1968 season in a slump. His blast off Lonborg turned out to be not only his last homer, but his last hit. Mantle went hitless in his final 20 at-bats. He finished the season hitting .237 with 18 home runs and 54 runs batted in. The Yankees fared a bit better, going 83-79 to finish above .500 for the first time since 1964. Even so, New York ended the season 20 games behind the Detroit Tigers.

MEMORIES OF MANTLE

A Sea of Waving Bats

It was Bat Day at Yankee Stadium in 1966 [June 19, Father's Day]. Back then they gave out real Louisville Sluggers and I was lucky enough to get a Mickey Mantle autograph model. The Stadium was packed.

Mickey, who was near the end of his career, stepped up to the plate, and without any prompting, everyone in the crowd spontaneously raised their bats in tribute to him. The Stadium was a sea of thousands of bats held high in the air. He responded by hitting a triple, which was really an accomplishment, since he couldn't run very well at that point in his career. The entire Stadium went absolutely nuts!

The next time Mickey came up, Bob Sheppard asked if everyone would raise their bats again so they could get a picture. It had been such an unplanned spontaneous moment that the photographers had missed getting a picture of the crowd.

The next day, the *Daily News* put a photograph of the bat salute on its back page, but I knew that was the "staged" picture. The "real" picture has been stored in my memory for more than 40 years.

— Tony Psomas, Westfield, New Jersey

During the winter of 1968 and 1969, Mantle had a feeling his career was over but he held off on a decision until spring arrived. One of the turning points for him, he told *Sport* magazine, was a dream—a nightmare, really—he had during the off-season. Around that time, all major league teams had to expose a certain number of players to the four 1969 expansion teams (the Kansas City Royals, Seattle Pilots, Montreal Expos, and San Diego Padres). Mantle dreamt that the Yankees left him unprotected and that the Royals took him.

The thought of playing for anyone but the Yankees helped him make his decision, as did his long history of injuries. So in February 1969, he arrived at the Yankees' camp in Fort Lauderdale a week early and let the team know of his intentions. And then, in an emotional press conference on March 1, he let the world know that he was through.

1965

Regular Season

Year	Age	G	AB	R	H	2B	3B	HR	RBI	SB	BB	SO	BA
1965	33	122	361	44	92	12	1	19	46	4	73	76	.255

Noteworthy

· On April 9, Mantle hits the first home run in Astrodome history in an exhibition game against the Houston Colt .45s (later Astros).

· Mantle starts the year with a bang: four homers in the Yankees' first 11 games. On defense, he's now playing left instead of centerfield.

· On May 15, Mantle thrills Yankee fans with an opposite-field 8th-inning homer off right-hander Dick Hall to break a 2-2 tie.

· The Yankees follow up their AL-pennant-winning season of 1964 with a 6th-place finish (77-85), while Mantle, affected by a bad hamstring and other nagging injuries, hits only .255.

· After the season, Mantle injures his shoulder playing touch football and contemplates retirement.

1966

Regular Season

Year	Age	G	AB	R	H	2B	3B	HR	RBI	SB	BB	SO	BA
1966	34	108	333	40	96	12	1	23	56	1	57	76	.288

Noteworthy

· Between June 28 and July 8, Mantle shows he's "still got it," connecting for nine homers in 11 days.

· Despite declining range and mobility, Mantle — back in centerfield — is still sure-handed; in 97 games, he commits no errors.

· On July 7, Mantle hits a three-run walk-off homer off Don McMahon to beat the Red Sox.

· On Aug. 26, with the Yankees down by a run in the bottom of the 9th inning, Mantle hits a pinch-hit two-run homer to win the game.

· The Yankees, however, sink to the cellar of the AL with a 70-89 record.

1967

Regular Season

Year	Age	G	AB	R	H	2B	3B	HR	RBI	SB	BB	SO	BA
1967	35	144	440	63	108	17	0	22	55	1	107	113	.245

Noteworthy

· His knees worn from multiple injuries over the years, Mantle moves to first base.

· On May 14, in the 3rd inning of a game against Baltimore at Yankee Stadium, Mantle hits his 500th career homer.

· He also hits two walk-off homers: a three-run blast off the Angels' Minnie Rojas on April 30 and a solo shot off the Tigers' Fred Gladding on June 24.

· Mantle plays in more games (144) than he has since 1961. He hits a career-low .245, but pitchers still respect his power, issuing him 107 walks.

· The Yankees climb a spot in the standings over 1966, but it's not much to cheer about; they finish at 72-90, in 9th place.

1968

Regular Season

Year	Age	G	AB	R	H	2B	3B	HR	RBI	SB	BB	SO	BA
1968	36	144	435	57	103	14	1	18	54	6	106	97	.237

Noteworthy

· Mantle plays in 144 games for the second year in a row, but his batting average sinks to .237.

· Still, pitchers respect his power; he draws 106 walks.

· On May 30, in the first game of a doubleheader, The Mick serves up a throwback performance, going 5 for 5 with two homers and five RBI.

· On Aug. 10, Mantle delivers his final multi-homer game, hitting two bombs off Twins lefty Jim Merritt.

· On Sept. 19 and 20, he hits his final two homers, both left-handed, off Denny McLain of Detroit and Jim Lonborg of Boston. The McLain homer was the "grooved" fastball that gave Mantle 535 in his career, surpassing Jimmie Foxx.

· In Mantle's last season, the Yankees rebound in the standings, going 83-79 and finishing in fifth place.

MANTLE QUITS

'I Just Can't Hit Any More'

The end came not with a bang but with an announcement. After 18 years in the majors and more than 2,400 games, Mantle, with manager Ralph Houk at his side, announced his retirement from baseball at a press conference in Fort Lauderdale, March 1, 1969.

Bruce Bennett Studios/Getty Images

Now It's Official
YEP, MICK QUITS

Mantle struggled with injuries throughout the 1965 season, causing the Yankees to wonder if their star might retire before they could properly pay tribute to him. To ward off any embarrassment, the Yankees honored Mantle on the eve on his 2,000th game, Sept. 18, 1965, in Yankee Stadium. Among the many dignitaries at the event were Senator Robert F. Kennedy and Mrs. Lou Gehrig. While the ceremony was a grand tribute to Mantle, the game that followed was not. Mantle went hitless in three at bats in a 4-3 loss to the Detroit Tigers.

MICKEY MANTLE DAY

Introduced to the Yankee Stadium crowd by former teammate and Yankee great Joe DiMaggio,
Mickey Mantle again demonstrated why he was a fan favorite with the following words:

"Thank you very much Joe. I think just to have the greatest baseball player I ever saw introduce me is tribute enough for me in one day. Today's game will be my 2,000th game with the Yankees. I've been very nervous in this ballpark many times in the last 15 years but never any more nervous than I am right now.

To name everyone who's helped me through my career would be impossible. So I'm gonna take this opportunity to say to them one and all, that I certainly appreciate everything they've done for me and hope that I've lived up to their expectations.

To have any kind of success in life I think you have someone behind you to push you ahead and to share it with if you're ever to obtain it. And I certainly have that in my wife Merlyn, little Mickey who's here, and I have three little boys at home that didn't get to come but they're watching on TV, David, Billy, and Danny. And also a wonderful mother who is here.

As you all know, all the donations for this day are turned over to the Hodgkin's disease Fund at St. Benton's Hospital. That was founded in the memory of my father who died of Hodgkin's disease. I wish he could have been here today. I know he would be just as proud and happy at what you all have done here as we are.

There's been a lot written in the last few years about the pain that I've played with. But I want you to know that when one of you fans, whether it's in New York or anywhere in the country, says "Hi Mick! How you feeling?" or "How are your legs?" it certainly makes it all worth it. All the people in New York, since I've been here, have been tremendous with me. Mr. Topping, all of my teammates, the press and the radio and the TV, have just been wonderful. I just wish I had 15 more years with you. Thank you very much."

Far away from the spotlight of baseball and the adulation of the New York sports scene, Mantle and his wife Merlyn relax with their young sons, Mickey Jr., Billy, Danny, and David in their home in Dallas. The role of father did not come easily for Mantle, who was not much of a family man. He was absent for much of his sons' childhood and had a well-deserved reputation as hard drinker.

John Dominis/Time Life Pictures/Getty Images

A stout, gregarious, back-slapping man, saloonkeeper Toots Shor reigned over midtown New York's nightlife for more than two decades. His restaurant was the favorite haunt of sports heroes, entertainers, cops, mobsters, politicians, and just about anyone famous in the city. Bing Crosby and Frank Sinatra would enter to applause. Jackie Gleason often held court at the bar. Notorious gangster Frank Costello could be found at the watering hole. And if you were a Yankee, Toots Shor's Restaurant was your place. Mickey Mantle, here with his wife, Merlyn, was the joint's most recognized regular. Although you could eat at his restaurant, Toots himself often wondered why you would bother when you could drink. During World War II, New York Mayor Jimmy Byrnes imposed a midnight curfew for all businesses in the city. The clubs were up in arms, but Toots calmed everyone down when he famously stated: "Any crum bum what can't get plastered by midnight just ain't tryin'."

John Dominis/Time & Life Pictures/Getty Images

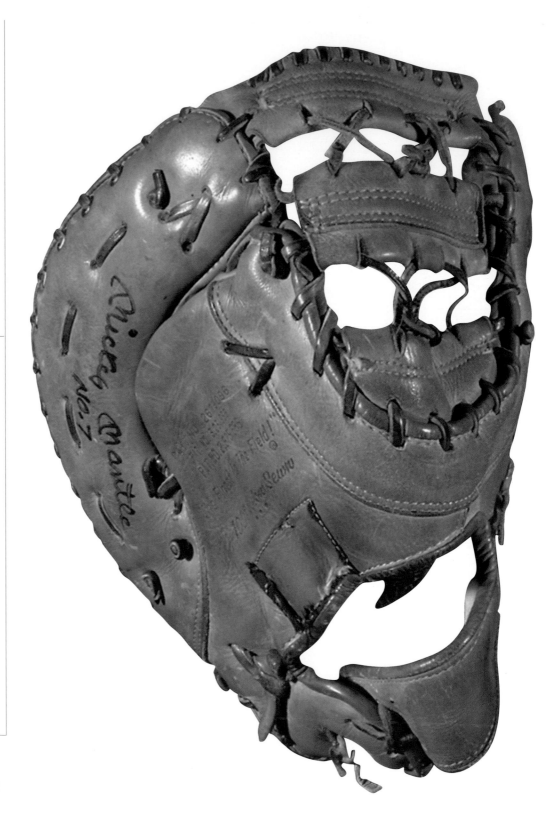

This 1966 Mantle game-worn road jersey (100% original and unaltered) sold at Heritage Auction Galleries for an astonishing $89,625 in April 2009. Mantle led the team with a .538 slugging percentage in 1966. That year would also mark the last time Mantle played in center field. He would move to first base in 1967 and use this glove.

As DiMaggio replaced Gehrig and Mantle replaced DiMaggio, Bobby Murcer was billed as the heir apparent to Mantle. The 19-year-old rookie Murcer poses with Mantle and Roger Maris in 1965 wearing a T-shirt of his heroes and new teammates. And while Murcer never fully lived up to the lofty expectations, he was a five-time All-Star and had a lifetime batting average of .277, with 252 home runs and 1,043 runs batted in. Murcer also played on "Mickey Mantle Day" alongside Mantle, calling the experience the "greatest thrill" of his career. Autographed by all three players, this charming 8 x 10-inch photograph sold at auction for $2,270.

Heritage Auction Galleries

Mantle and his good friend and teammate Whitey Ford celebrated many milestones together, including induction into the Baseball Hall of Fame in 1974. Signed by the Yankees as an amateur free agent in 1947, Ford went 9-1 in his first season in the majors in 1950. His rookie year was a sign of things to come. The lefthander finished his 16-year career with 236 wins against 106 defeats and a sparkling 2.75 earned run average. From 1950 to 1964, he pitched in 11 World Series, helping the Yankees win eight titles during that span.

Heritage Auction Galleries

When Mantle decided to retire from the Yankees he did so with a heavy heart. But he also left as one of the greatest players in the history of the storied franchise. In addition to hitting 536 lifetime home runs, he led the American League in homers four times and was chosen as the league's Most Valuable Player three times. Along with his Triple Crown season in 1956, he played on 12 pennant-winning and seven World Series-winning teams. He still holds the all-time record for home runs in World Series play (18) as well as numerous other World Series records. Mantle was a symbol of the Yankees and their greatness. In 1974 he was elected to baseball's Hall of Fame in his first year on the ballot.

John Dominis//Time Life Pictures/
Getty Images

Mantle's 1969 New York Yankees contract went unsigned, a stark symbol of the end of a remarkable career.

Guernsey's

Mantle wipes his eyes as 61,000 fans at Yankee Stadium give him an eight-minute ovation on Mickey Mantle Day on June 8, 1969.

NY Daily News Archive via Getty Images

chapter eight
Life After Baseball

FACING:
After playing baseball almost his entire life, Mantle struggled to fill the void that the game left.

Ronald C. Modra/Sports Imagery/ Getty Images

RIGHT:
A Mantle-autographed baseball noting his Hall of Fame induction date.

Heritage Auction Galleries

WHEN MICKEY MANTLE RETIRED in March 1969, the Yankees set out to honor him with a fittingly dramatic celebration. On June 8, 1969, the team hosted Mickey Mantle Day at Yankee Stadium. Longtime announcer Mel Allen introduced Mantle this way: "...I'm terribly privileged to have the honor to once again call from the dugout one of the all-time Yankee greats… the magnificent Yankee… the great No. 7, Mickey Mantle!"

The 61,000 fans in attendance gave Mantle a stirring reception: some eight minutes of spirited, appreciative applause that—for those who were there or who watched it on television—seemed to go on for hours. Finally, Mantle stepped to the microphone.

"When I walked into this stadium 18 years ago, I felt much the same way I do right now. I don't have words to describe how I felt then or how I feel now, but I'll tell you one thing: baseball was real good to me and playing 18 years in Yankee Stadium for you folks is the best thing that could ever happen to a ballplayer. Now to think that the Yankees are retiring my number 7 with numbers 3, 4, and 5 tops off everything that I could ever wish for.

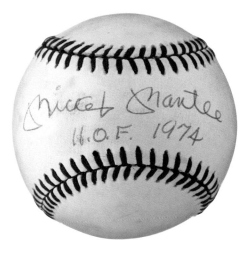

Although he claimed working on TV was "easier than hitting a baseball," Mantle's television career was short-lived.
Michael Ochs Archives/Getty Images

The "test" didn't actually turn into anything more than an experiment. Mantle was well received by fans, but he never felt comfortable working in front of a camera, so after the season, he walked away from broadcasting.

Then he tried coaching. Mantle had a standing offer from Yankee manager Ralph Houk to join his staff. On August 29, 1970, he gave it a whirl, returning to pinstripes to coach first base—but only during the middle three innings of Yankee games. After a week, he realized that the role wasn't for him; besides, he knew he was there strictly as a drawing card for a struggling young Yankee team. Again, Mick moved on.

Mantle did discover that there was great demand for him as a public speaker. Shortly after retiring, he got paid the princely sum of $500 for a speech; in the two-plus decades that followed, he would travel around the nation making personal appearances, and his fees would rise into four-figure and ultimately five-figure sums.

In 1974, Mickey Mantle received baseball's ultimate individual honor: induction into the Hall of Fame. He became only the seventh player in history elected in his first year of eligibility, receiving 322 votes out of 365 ballots, or 88 percent. At the time, it was the ninth-highest percentage in four decades of voting. (Looking back at the results, though, you have to wonder about the 43 voters who circled "no" on their ballots.) The fact that Mantle's good friend Whitey Ford was elected to the Hall in 1974—it was his second year of eligibility—made the honor even sweeter.

Mantle, in his Hall of Fame acceptance speech, reminisced about his life in baseball, starting with his early days, when his dad first started him on the path of switch-hitting: "…[H]e taught me, he and his father, to switch-hit at a real young age, when I first started to learn how to play ball. And my dad always told me if I could hit both ways, when I got ready to go to the major leagues, that I would have a better chance of playing. And believe it or not, the year that I came to the Yankees is when Casey Stengel started to platoon everybody."

He also showed the self-effacing humor for which he was known: "I would really like to thank you [Commissioner Bowie Kuhn, who referenced Mickey's hitting accomplishments] for leaving out those strikeouts. He gave all those records, but he didn't

MEMORIES OF MANTLE

A True Show-Stopper

I had the experience of meeting Mickey Mantle in 1994 while I was working for the sports memorabilia publication Tuff Stuff. Mickey agreed to do an autograph signing appearance at our annual Tuff Stuff Classic card show in June on behalf of Upper Deck Trading Cards. A few of our staff members were asked by his agent to join them for dinner the night before the show. I had no idea what to expect, but assumed a sports legend of his caliber would have quite a big ego. In reality, he had a sense of humor that I could appreciate—lots of playful banter and heavy sarcasm. He enjoyed holding court at the head of the table, cracking jokes with our group and the restaurant staff. The next day he was ready for work—signing autographs, shaking hands, and taking photos with hundreds of adoring fans. It was the best Tuff Stuff Classic we ever had.

A few months later, I joined Mickey and his agent for dinner while we were all in Pittsburgh for the All-Star Game. It was just the three of us, sitting at a corner table in the hotel bar. Mickey was very personable and I appreciated that he remembered meeting me in Richmond a few months earlier. While I know I should have felt privileged for having such exclusive access to this icon, the dinner was so casual I didn't even think about it.

Even under normal circumstances, Mickey might have had trouble enjoying a meal in public without being interrupted. That weekend, though, Pittsburgh was teeming with baseball royalty, and fans were on high alert. Shortly after we had ordered our food, a man in his 40s strolled over to the table and stood in front of Mickey with his jaw hanging open. It was a very awkward moment, because the man didn't say a word; he just stared at Mickey.

After what seemed like an eternity, the man simply said, "You're my hero," and he continued to stare at Mickey with an adoring look in his eye. At that point someone needed to do something, so Mickey reached into his pocket and pulled out an autographed postcard. Mickey gave a forced smile as he handed the autograph to the man, who was still being polite but was clearly uncomfortable. Finally the man walked away and Mickey went back to trying to enjoy his dinner—before the next fan interrupted….

—Molly Sapienza, Charlotte, North Carolina

doubt exist even to this day. When the FBI's Operation Bullpen in 2000 collared a forgery ring said to have produced $100 million in bogus memorabilia, fake Mantle items were among the most prevalent.

It's yet another tribute to his stature that signed Mantle material emerged from that turning point largely unbowed. While such a debacle might have shattered the market for another player's autograph, the demand for Mantle-signed pieces continues. And it was never more in evidence than three years after Operation Bullpen.

On December 8, 2003, Guernsey's conducted an auction at Madison Square Garden of material from the Mantle estate. Total take from the auction: more than $4 million. Mickey's 1957 MVP Award alone sold for $321,000, while his 1956 Silver Bat trophy (for winning the batting title) brought $312,000 and his 1962 World Series ring drew $162,000. Proving that signatures with good provenance can pack a lot of wallop, Mantle's individual player contracts from 1949-69 sold for a total of almost $700,000.

In the years that followed, Mantle memorabilia continued to draw hefty prices. A few examples:

• The first baseball Mantle ever hit for a home run in the major leagues sold for $189,750 at Sotheby's in 2004. Mantle himself had saved the ball and inscribed it ("My first H.R. in the Majors, May 1, 1951, 4:50 p.m. Chicago" and "6th inning off Randy Gumpert"). He later donated it to the Little League Museum in Baxter Springs, Kansas.

• A home Yankee jersey (unsigned) worn by Mantle during the 1963 season sold for $143,400 at Heritage Auction Galleries in 2004.

• A game-worn home jersey from Mantle's 1955 season sold for $125,330 at SCP Auctions in 2010. (The jersey included Mantle's autograph).

• A Hillerich & Bradsby 1958 World Series model game bat used by Mantle (and later autographed) brought $91,000 at Sotheby's in 2008.

• A Louisville Slugger 125 model bat issued to Mantle for use in the 1960 World Series (and likely used by Mickey in that memorable series against the Pirates) sold for $46,000 at Hunt Auctions in 2006.

Mantle, while he was alive, didn't consider himself the lead dog in the collectibles market. That would have been two other outfielders. "Right now, Joe DiMaggio and Ted Williams—not me—are the kings of the memorabilia business," he said in a 1994 interview. "DiMaggio gets $400 for a baseball, and I get $100. So I wouldn't call myself the king."

While DiMaggio and Williams memorabilia has always been highly sought by collectors, Mantle is the one who made the greatest post-Babe impact on the hobby. And it all started, really, with his first Topps baseball card. The striking hand-colored portrait of a baby-faced yet powerful-looking Mantle issued on a small piece of cardboard in the innocent summer of 1952 had kids tearing into Topps packs all summer long—and they'd repeat the practice right up until his last card as a player came out: 1969 Topps No. 500.

"Mickey gave life to the trading card industry on three occasions," said Marty Appel, a former public relations man for the Yankees and author of more than a dozen baseball books. "First, he was the great 'chase card' when the modern baseball card era began, in the early 1950s, because he was the most popular player of this time. Second, the high-dollar sales of his vintage cards in the late 1970s and early 1980s gave life to the weekend card show industry. And finally, his 'memorial' cards after his passing in 1995 helped to rescue the trading card industry, which at the time was in the wake of baseball's 1994 strike."

Ironically, it was a mass-produced card created as one of Mickey Mantle's final wishes—in the weeks before he lost his battle with cancer in August 1995—that has made the greatest impact in "the real world." A widely distributed organ donation card bearing Mickey's likeness and facsimile signature would encourage thousands of fans to participate, to fill out a card and carry it in a wallet or purse.

If that were his only legacy—that desire to help others stricken with his disease—it would be enough to open the pearly gates for anyone. Of course, Mickey Mantle himself wouldn't see it that way. He frequently told the story about how he envisioned St. Peter greeting him at the gates of heaven after he died and saying, "Mick, we've checked your records carefully, and we're afraid we can't let you in. Sorry. But before you go, God wants to know if you could just sign these six dozen baseballs."

Cardboard classic

The root of Mantle's popularity among collectors can be traced to his 1952 Topps baseball card (No. 311). Boys of the early 1950s wanted that card more than any other, and when baby boomers began chasing their childhoods in the 1980s, that card helped to fuel the astronomical growth of baseball card collecting. Mantle's 1952 Topps is frequently referred to as his "rookie card," but that honor actually belongs to his 1951 Bowman. Even so, there's no question that it's the 1952 Topps that spurred the baseball card hobby. As sports memorabilia expert Simeon Lipman put it, "Topps was just starting out—1952 was its first major set and its first full-color set. Those 1952s and 1953s are totally different than anything made before them. They were bigger physically, for example, so kids had an easier time holding them in their hands. Plus, the 1952 Mantle card was double-printed, and there was a reason for that: there was already a demand for Mantle stuff."

The '52 Topps Mantle has a book value of around $30,000, but top-condition, high-grade examples can sell for as much as 10 times that amount. The '51 Bowman Mantle has been gradually rising in price over the years and currently sits at around $10,000. Again, a high-grade example can exceed book value many times over; in 2007, a Near-Mint/Mint 1951 Bowman card of Mantle sold for $160,000 at Mastro Auctions. One factor behind the status of the 1952 Topps Mantle is a classic bit of hobby lore. Topps issued its high series so late in the summer of 1952 that sales were a dismal disappointment. The company tried, without much success, to unload the leftover stock of high-number cards through carnivals and arrangements with various toy companies over the next several years. By 1960, storage space was deemed more important than the cards in question, so Topps' Sy Berger loaded the cases onto a barge and dumped them into the Atlantic Ocean. It's a great story—and true, by Berger's own admission—that adds to the mystique surrounding Mantle's '52 Topps card.

Mantle's 1952 Topps Card

Mantle's 1951 Bowman Card

MICKEY CHARLES MANTLE

Outfielder
Bats: Both   Throws: Right
Ht: 5'11"   Wt: 195
Born: Spavinaw, OK   10/20/31

Playing Record
1951-1968 New York Yankees

Games	2401
At Bats	8102
Hits	2415
Doubles	344
Triples	72
Home Runs	536
Runs	1677
Runs Batted In	1509
Batting Average	.298

Elected to the Hall of Fame

INDUCTION DAY
August 12, 1974
Cooperstown, New York

Mickey Mantle

© 1988 TV Sports Mailbag, Pleasantville, New York   Limited Edition of 1000

Mantle and Whitey Ford were as excited as children to be inducted into the Baseball Hall of Fame together in 1974.

Diamond Images/Getty Images

EDWARD CHARLES FORD
"Whitey"

Pitcher
Bats: Left   Throws: Left
Ht: 5'10"   Wt: 178 lbs
Born: New York, N.Y.   10/21/28

Playing Record
1950-67 New York Yankees

Games	498
Won	236
Lost	106
Percentage	.690
Games Started	438
Games Completed	156
Innings Pitched	3170.1
Hits	2766
Walks	1086
Strike Outs	1956
ERA	2.75

Hall of Fame

INDUCTION DAY
August 11, 1974
Cooperstown, New York

Whitey Ford

© 1989 TV Sports Mailbag, Pleasantville, New York   #15   Limited Edition of 1000

Long after their playing days were over, Mantle and Whitey Ford remained friends. Here the two are shown at a baseball fantasy camp in the 1980s in Haines City, Florida.

Ronald C. Modra/Sports Imagery/Getty Images

When Mantle was honored June 8, 1969, during Mickey Mantle Day at Yankee Stadium, he said he finally understood how Lou Gehrig could have considered himself "the luckiest man on the face of the earth" 30 years earlier at his own goodbye to the Bronx. This stunning display compiles all of the important components from that summer of 1969. Clockwise from top left: a wire photograph announcing Mantle's retirement; a "Sport Magazine" doing the same; a signed program from the event with "No. 7" notation; a photograph of the event; an oversized button sold at the Stadium that day; a very tough ticket stub for the event; and a souvenir pennant sold that day. An engraved plaque at bottom center makes note of all of the major milestones of Mantle's storied Hall of Fame career, with career statistics. At 35 x 40 inches, this framed salute to Mantle sold for $1,314.50 at auction.

Heritage Auction Galleries

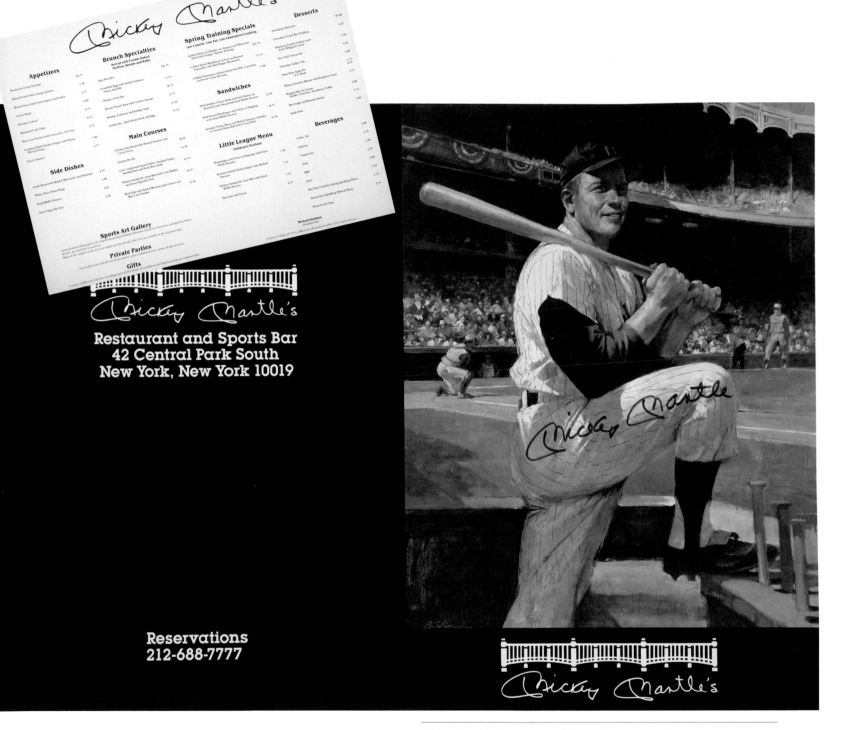

Mickey Mantle's Restaurant and Sports Bar was one of many businesses Mantle dabbled in after retiring. The establishment still stands at 42 Central Park South, New York.

Heritage Auction Galleries

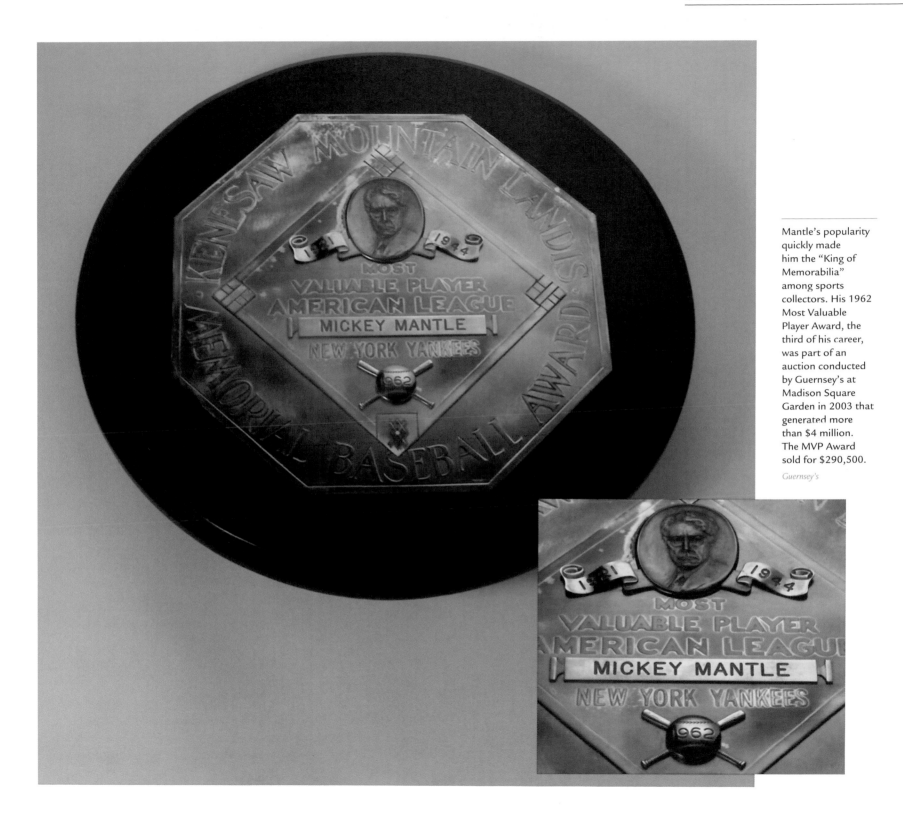

Mantle's popularity quickly made him the "King of Memorabilia" among sports collectors. His 1962 Most Valuable Player Award, the third of his career, was part of an auction conducted by Guernsey's at Madison Square Garden in 2003 that generated more than $4 million. The MVP Award sold for $290,500.

Guernsey's

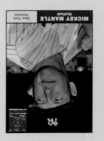

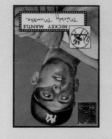

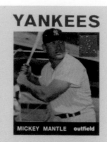

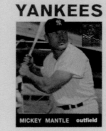

To honor The Mick after his death, Topps re-released every standard-issue Mantle card it created. This is a rare uncut sheet of those cards, issued in 1996.

Fortunately, Mantle's irreverent sense of humor followed him throughout his retirement as evidenced by this autographed golf photograph. He stands to the side as his golf buddy tees off, waving his finger in his direction. The inscription explains Mantle's maneuver, reading, "Jim, My zap didn't work, you lucky shit. Mickey Mantle."

Heritage Auction Galleries

For some, the memories of Mantle remain as fresh today as when they were first created decades ago. In those memories, The Mick never aged and always came up with the big hit.

Heritage Auction Galleries

Mickey Mantle for the Soul

LOOKING BACK AT MICKEY MANTLE'S LIFE AND CAREER, we see an athlete who seemed destined to become a star on baseball's most storied franchise. We see a unique player who covered center field with the best of them, who produced prodigious home runs as well as perfectly finessed drag bunts, who ran like the wind. We also see a personality and appearance that played "just right" in 1950s America—a shy country boy with blond hair, a muscular build, and friendly features. And has there ever been a better name for a baseball player? (Mickey used to joke that he's glad his father didn't give him Hall of Fame catcher Mickey Cochrane's real first name or we'd have heard, "Now batting… Gordon Mantle.")

Mickey brought fans to their feet throughout his career, whether he was cranking out a tape-measure blast, striking out or, as it was at the end of his career, merely emerging from the dugout to hit. Yet his story is also a tragic one. At 63, he died too young; how many years did alcohol take from his life? His career, too, was shorter than it should have been, compared to today's standards. Despite setting a record for games played by a Yankee (2,401), Mantle lost far too many games to injuries; what if he had taken rehabilitation and physical therapy more seriously? On a personal level, he was the first to admit he was far from perfect. Drinking and its disastrous effects caused untold levels of pain for his family; regrettably, he admitted in the last book to which he contributed, *A Hero for Life*, he couldn't call himself a good family man.

Yet his fans, his legions of fans, were and are forgiving of Mantle. He's still a hero, and not just for the awesome home runs and dramatic clutch hits during his 18 seasons. Mickey's most heroic act was in his final days. As his battle with cancer became hopeless, he took responsibility and expressed deep regret for wasting a lot of years. Who can forget the press conference in July 1995 when a dying Mantle pointed to himself and said, "This is a role model—don't be like me."

Mickey Mantle left us with that image, that moment where he came to grips with his failures. He was human, after all. Yet we still come back to the pinstriped wonder, the ballplayer that provided a generation of fans with unforgettable thrills. Throughout these pages, we've sprinkled "Mantle Memories" as related by fans who grew up watching him play. The essays here capture the special connection Mantle forged with so many fans around the nation—fans who won't ever forget No. 7.

Mantle was the focus of photographers and fans alike during his transcendent 1956 season when he won baseball's Triple Crown; the Yankees won the World Series; and he was named American League Most Valuable Player.

Heritage Auction Galleries

A Voice from the Mantle Generation

By Daniel Sullivan, Bennington, New Hampshire

Growing up in New York in a family full of Brooklyn Dodgers fans, I knew I had to be different. So in 1954, when I was 7, I started rooting for the Yankees. While my family members' favorite players were Reese, Hodges, and Snider (father, mother, and older brother, respectively), mine was Mickey Mantle.

I was an avid radio fan and amateur box-score keeper, so I stayed glued to the transistor on summer days listening to Red Barber (who also had recently transferred from Dodgers to Yankees). More than a few times during that 1954 season, I heard The Ol' Redhead *back, back, back*-ing opposing outfielders to no avail as The Mick sailed another one over the wall.

My switch of allegiance to the Yankees in 1954 paid no immediate dividends. While the Dodgers didn't make the World Series that year, neither did the Yankees, despite winning more than 100 games (the Cleveland Indians won 111!). And in 1955, the full weight of my sins came crashing down upon me: the Dodgers—after losing to the Yankees in 1941, '47, '49, '52, and '53—finally won the World Series. Even worse, Mantle was injured and played in only three games, hitting one home run.

Maybe it was because "Dem Bums" had finally beaten the Bronx Bombers that my father felt magnanimous enough in 1956 to take me (and my less-enthusiastic brother) to my first-ever game at Yankee Stadium. We had visited Ebbets Field a number of times, but this was my first trip uptown to (their) "enemy" territory. I was completely overwhelmed by how enormous the place was.

After sitting down in our ground-level seats off the left-field line, I gazed toward the monuments dedicated to Babe Ruth and Lou Gehrig. They were in the field of play in Death Valley, the deepest part of center field, but they seemed a mile away. I remember looking up at the right-field upper deck, whose façade seemed like some impossible skyscraper that only Mickey Mantle could ever reach.

Despite all my normally meticulous scorekeeping, the details from that day are sketchy, though I know we played the Detroit Tigers, we won, and The Mick didn't hit any homers. It was the Stadium I remember most—its vast greenness bordered by dark walls lettered with gigantic numbers, like 457 and 461 in left-center and center field.

Thankfully, 1956 turned out to be a better year than the previous two. Mick had that Triple Crown season (.353, 52 homers, 130 RBI), and the Yankees took revenge on the Dodgers. Better still, my family, now on Long Island, had a TV set. My biggest thrill was watching Mickey Mantle hit a home run in Game 4.

As I went through junior high school, the Yankees kept winning and The Mick remained awesome. He had big years in 1957 and 1958, when the Yankees split a pair of World Series with the Milwaukee Braves. To copy The Mick, I had taken up switch-hitting, but around that time, I realized my own baseball career was about to peak—somewhere between Little League all-star and Babe Ruth also-ran.

The 1960s changed everything. Even the Yankees. Even Mickey Mantle. I should have realized that the 1960 World Series meant something more than an aberration. The Yankees destroyed the

Mantle always stood tall in the eyes of his fans, even at the end of his playing days when his quest to hit .300 came up short.

Focus on Sport/Getty Images

Pirates in six games, statistically speaking, but the Series remained tied at 3. Mantle kept saving the Yankees' bacon with clutch hits (three homers, 11 RBI, and a .400 average in the series), but the Yankees fell to Bill Mazeroski's thunderbolt in the 9th inning.

The Yankees came back with a vengeance in 1961, when the M&M Show captivated all of us. I rooted for Mantle and cried "unfair!" because Maris got to bat third in the order and enjoy all those strikes from pitchers who feared the Mighty Mick in the cleanup spot. But what I remember most about 1961 was this: Mantle was breaking down—physically—as the season wore on. Of course he couldn't win the home run race; he could hardly walk. And a severe hip infection cost him crucial games down the stretch. But he did stand on that top dugout step and root for Maris to accomplish what only he was destined to do: eclipse Babe Ruth.

Mantle didn't contribute much in the Yankees' manhandling of the Reds in the 1961 World Series or in their win over the Giants in the 1962 Series, although he did win the MVP that season despite missing nearly 40 games. After another abbreviated, injury-plagued regular season in 1963, Mantle again contributed little when the Dodgers swept the Yanks in the World Series.

While The Mick seemed to fade in the early 1960s, I noticed something about him. Actually, I was probably noticing something about myself. Because I had Mantle baseball cards dating to 1954, I could always quote his height (5'11") and weight (198 pounds, give or take a few). He had always looked huge—tall, broad shoulders rippling in pinstripes and forearms like fireplace logs. But in a game I attended at the Stadium in my senior year in high school, 1964, my girlfriend's father got us wonderful box seats near first base. Suddenly, I realized The Mick wasn't all that tall (by this time, I had nearly three inches on him). And he looked—maybe only slightly—ordinary.

He didn't hit any homers that day to restore my hero-worship crush, but he did have a resurgent season overall, hitting 35 homers and driving in 111 runs. And in the most exciting World Series I had ever seen (even though we lost a heartbreaker in seven games to the Cardinals), Mick came through like the golden boy of the past: a walk-off homer in Game 3, back-to-back homers with Maris in Game 6, and a valiant three-run blast in Game 7 that couldn't quite erase the Cardinals' early lead.

Mantle played four more years, but they clearly were the most dispiriting of his career. There was a noticeable limp in his gait, and the most graceful of center fielders now played first base. And the Yankees sunk in the standings.

I didn't pay much attention to Mantle those last four years—not until late 1968, when I did take in a few final Yankees games. And reverting to the old box-score-keeper and junior statistician I had been as a kid, I began charting Mantle's lifetime batting average. If he had retired after 1967, he would have had a .302 career average. But now .300 looked doubtful. If Mick had been "only" a slugger, maybe it wouldn't have mattered. But he had always been much more than a power hitter: there were bunt singles, singles stretched into doubles, and doubles into triples.

Alas, there was no miracle of 1968. The box score for Sept. 28, 1968 shows Mantle going 0 for 1 in his last game. His batting average after more than 8,000 at-bats will forever read .298. The Mick deserved better.

[Sullivan is a longtime magazine and book editor whose writing has appeared in *Yankee*, *The Daily Racing Form*, and *The New York Times*, among other publications.]

Mantle poses next to his old uniform just prior to a ceremony where his jersey number was officially retired during ceremonies June 8, 1969.

B Bennett/Getty Images

Mickey Mantle Day Memories

By Nate Salant, Birmingham, Alabama

I saw Mickey Mantle play when I was a child in the mid-late 1960s. The very first game I went to, Mantle hit a home run that a woman sitting in front of me caught with her baseball glove—right in front of my face. We were in the upper deck in right field in the old Yankee Stadium, and all I remember was that ball coming right at me—it was frightening for a kid!

My greatest Mantle memory, though, dates to Sunday, June 8, 1969, the day the Yankees retired Mickey's No. 7. Somewhere, I have the whole thing on an old spool tape that worked in a tape recorder my parents bought for my bar mitzvah lessons. My dad was not happy, to say the least, when I brought that recorder to Yankee Stadium in 1969.

Anyway, I remember the way Mantle started his speech: he surprised Joe DiMaggio by presenting him with a plaque "that would hang out there on the center field wall..." (DiMaggio did not expect it and responded by saying, "This is a complete surprise to me. I had no idea this was going to happen. I'd just like to say that I'm out there in great company.")

Mantle then proceeded to utter these timeless words: "I've often wondered how a man who knew he was going to die could stand out here and say he was the luckiest man in the world—but now I think I know how Lou Gehrig felt."

In 1978, I was covering the Yankees at their home games as I worked on my first book. I was there all the time, and on Old-Timers Day that season, I got to meet Maris, Mantle, DiMaggio, Raschi, and just about everyone else. I was edgy about approaching Mantle and Maris, but Mickey was wonderful—friendly, easy to talk to, enthusiastic about answering my questions. Maris was even better.

In 1979, when the book was on the market, I was delighted to present Mantle, Maris, and Whitey Ford with copies. And you know what? Mickey seemed genuinely appreciative. I couldn't help but ask him to autograph a copy for me, so he signed his name underneath DiMaggio's signature on the title page of a book I kept for myself.

[Salant is author of *This Date in New York Yankees History* (1979, 1981, and 1983) and *Superstars, Stars & Just Plain Heroes* (1982), both published by Stein & Day.]

Mantle hit 536 home runs in his career, which may have helped save at least one life in a most unusual way.

Mickey Saved My Brother's Life

By Mike Hankinson, Unionville, Pennsylvania

Watching Mickey Mantle step up to the plate was the most electrifying spectacle imaginable for a 10- or 11-year-old kid. Except for those occasional at-bats where we now know he may well have had a hangover and just looked plain clumsy, every at-bat was special. Some of his strikeouts were as memorable as his homers. And when he hit one out, his shy grin made every kid want to be a better player.

The first time I saw Mick play in person was in 1966, when I was 10. My father took us up to a night game, and we rode the #6 train to Jerome Avenue. To this day, I recall that first glimpse, from inside the train, of Yankee Stadium, seeing the dark brown dirt, the green infield grass, and the lights (only for a split second).

At the time, Mickey was in his "twilight" years and was less potent but nonetheless a living legend. When he was healthy, you could sense—even from the grandstands at Yankee Stadium—his power and speed. All it took was a look at his forearms and his wide back, or his amazing quickness when he left the batter's box. Mickey Mantle was, as much as Willie Mays, "The Natural."

One unforgettable and personal memory of Mickey was the day he saved my brother's life. When I was 11, we were about to head out on a family vacation from New York City to South Carolina. My big brother, unbeknownst to me, decided to sit in front of a sun lamp to get a base tan, but he fell asleep under the lamp. Just before Mickey's first at-bat, I started shouting and running around the apartment to fetch my brother; I didn't want him to miss The Mick. I found him under the lamp and woke him up, and we both ran in to watch Mickey hit.

By early morning, my brother's face and torso were blistered. He had suffered severe burns, with his face eventually pruning up, in terrible pain, with a couple of layers of skin peeling off. We often wonder what would have happened if Mickey Mantle had not come to bat that night. I might have lost my brother, best friend, and supreme Mantle imitator.

In one of the most dramatic moments of his career, Mantle reaches home plate after hitting a walk-off home run off knuckleballer Barney Schultz to lead the Yankees past the St. Louis Cardinals 2-1 in Game 3 of the 1964 World Series.

Heritage Auction Galleries

A Hero 'til the End

By David Barmak, Washington, D.C.

I grew up in the Bronx in the 1950s and Mickey Mantle was my hero. And I mean that quite literally. I worshipped him. Was it the speed? The titanic home runs? The way he carried himself? The fact (if I could even discern it then) that he was at once a ballplayer with seemingly supernatural gifts and a man with substantial and very human flaws? I don't know. But I idolized him.

For one birthday (I would guess when I was 5 or 6), my parents bought me a Yankee uniform. My mother bought an iron-on patch, cut it into No. 7, and ironed it onto the back. To this day, I have a picture of me in that uniform imitating Mantle's right-handed stance—and sporting a Mickey-like crew cut.

I also have a very distinct memory of sitting on my bed a couple of years later listening to a game on the radio. When Mickey came to bat, I silently hoped he would hit a homer for me, on my birthday—and he did! I ran to the kitchen to tell my mother; I was beside myself with excitement. I don't remember the year, but the stats show he homered on my birthday in each of the 1959, 1960, and 1961 seasons, the years I turned 7, 8 and 9 years of age.

In 1961 my parents took me to a bungalow colony in the Catskills for the summer and I followed the Mantle/Maris home run chase daily in *The New York Times*. I was crushed when injuries in September ended Mickey's bid to break Babe Ruth's record.

When Maris hit his 60th and 61st homers, those moments were bittersweet. Breaking Babe's record was a feat that Mickey, the better power hitter, should have accomplished… or at least that was the perspective of a disappointed 9-year-old.

Perhaps my most memorable Mantle moment was in 1964. I was watching Game 3 of the World Series with my father. It was tied in the bottom of the 9th inning and Mantle was coming to bat against the knuckleballer Barney Schultz. I remember saying, "Mickey hits the knuckleball good." What I was really thinking but afraid to say out loud was: "Mickey is gonna hit one. I just know it." And he did. First pitch. Upper deck. Right field. Game over! Today it's called a walk-off homer. History shows it was The Mick's 16th World Series home run, beating Ruth's record.

There were other great (perhaps even greater) players then: Mays, Musial, Aaron and others. But somehow they never achieved the heroic stature of Mickey Mantle.

A few years ago, I was watching a TV special about Mickey and his painful final illness, and he showed dignity as the end approached. When he owned up to the damage his drinking and carousing had done, I cried like a baby. My wife, who grew up overseas and didn't know much about baseball, let alone about Mickey Mantle, finally understood: Mickey Mantle was, truly, my hero.

Larger Than Life

By Eric Trill, Boca Raton, Florida

I was born in New York in 1950, and Mickey Mantle was the one constant of my youth that energized and engaged me from around age 7 until I packed up and headed off to college at the close of his career. For six months out of every year while growing up, I watched him on TV, read every sports article about him, and traveled to Yankee Stadium many times to marvel at this larger-than-life historical figure who had such a mesmerizing hold on me. It was as if I knew back then that I was watching something very special and rare, and that I needed to experience and treasure it closely for as long as possible.

At Mickey Mantle's funeral in 1995, Bob Costas delivered an eloquent eulogy in which he spoke about boys building a shrine to their baseball hero where a candle forever burns. Now, at age 60, I can tell you that my candle in front of my Mickey Mantle "shrine" burns as brightly today as it did over 50 years ago, when No. 7 was the hero of New York and baseball fans everywhere.

I once saw it written that Mickey was "the most loved and feared" baseball player of his era. I'm glad I grew up in that era. Giants like Mickey Mantle don't come around very often.

Mantle caused a stir even while watching the action from the on-deck circle, as he does here while Roger Maris hits during World Series action against St. Louis in 1964.

Marvin E. Newman/Sports Illustrated/Getty Images

With Mantle at the
plate, greatness was
simply a swing away.

Robert Riger/Getty Images)

At Any Moment, a Great Moment

By Corey J. Ayling, Minneapolis, Minnesota

I was born in 1957 and didn't start watching the Yankees until they fell on hard times in 1965. But I do remember that whenever Mickey Mantle came to the plate, he would receive a tremendous ovation. It was different from anything Reggie or Jeter received because it happened with *every* at-bat. In our home, anyone who was not watching the game would be called in to see Mickey Mantle hit. It was never "Mantle" or "The Mick," either; it was always both names said together: "Mickey Mantle," the greatest baseball name ever.

With Mantle, the anticipation was that he could do something tremendous, especially if he was hitting right-handed. If he came up batting righty, there would be an extra level of excitement because we all knew he could absolutely kill the ball.

An important part of the appeal of Mantle was that he was a link to the era when the Yankees won routinely. Late in his career, I got used to watching the Yankees struggle, and there was really no hope that they would win. For me, it was difficult to imagine the Yankees ever being a powerhouse team. But the sight of Mantle was living proof of a great era.

I remember watching games with my father, who would yell at the TV whenever Phil Linz made an error and who would tell me that the Yankees actually once were a great team and that it was a disgrace what they were fielding now. Mantle represented everything that was once great, and my peers and I unquestioningly accepted him as the greatest living ballplayer. In fact, when Joe DiMaggio was introduced by that moniker at Old Timers' games, I couldn't understand it; I resented the old guy and loved Mantle!

The greatest Yankee? Joe DiMaggio or Mickey Mantle? For many, there was no debate at all: It was Mantle.

Years after Mantle's playing days ended, he managed to make an impact on a fan's career just as it was getting started.

One Day with My Idol

By Dave Fogelson, South Orange, New Jersey

I once spent a day with "The Mick," my boyhood idol from the 1950s and '60s. It was in the mid-1970s and I was working in Philadelphia on a nationally syndicated TV program, *Greatest Sports Legends*. Paul Hornung was the show's host and conducted the interviews. It was a dream-come-true job for any young sports fan.

Mickey flew into Philadelphia the night before filming, and I eagerly volunteered to pick him up at the airport. Back then, you could actually go to the gate to meet passengers. It was obvious Mick had had a few during the flight. He'd also struck up an acquaintance with one of the stewardesses. I introduced myself and said I'd be driving him to the hotel. He didn't expect to be greeted by someone from the show and wasn't happy about it. He was pretty surly but got into the car with his friend. I didn't care about his demeanor. I was driving Mickey Mantle!

I picked him up at the hotel the next morning, and he couldn't have been more cordial. He did a great interview and happily obliged me (and others) by signing autographs. He had beautiful, flowing penmanship. I still have the ball he signed: "To Dave, My best wishes to a great friend. Mickey Mantle."

Growing up in northwest New Jersey, we'd get to go to Yankee Stadium about three or four times a season. These were the only opportunities we had to see our heroes and that magnificent baseball cathedral in color. It was something you'd look forward to weeks in advance and an experience you tried to keep ingrained in your mind for weeks afterward.

A number of times I went to the Stadium, unfortunately, Mick wasn't in the line-up. In those instances, you prayed he'd get to pinch-hit. I've been present for some memorable home runs hit at the Stadium (Chris Chambliss' walk-off vs. Kansas City to clinch the pennant in 1977, for example), but I regret never seeing The Mick hit one out in person.

Those were simpler times for viewing sports, and I believe much better times. Within the "cozy confines" of The Big Ballpark in the Bronx, you'd focus on just the two teams, and enjoy the iconic voice of Bob Sheppard over the PA, organ music between innings, and the sound of vendors hawking Yankee yearbooks (75 cents), hot dogs, and Ballantine beer. It has never gotten any better than that.

No one hit home runs farther than Mantle. And no one enjoys telling just how far they went than his fans.

A Heat-Seeking Missile

By Dennis Piermont, Dayton, Ohio

I grew up in New York City in the 1950s and saw Mickey Mantle many, many times. One of them was on June 14, 1964, when the White Sox were playing at Yankee Stadium. Chicago was up 1-0 when Mickey led off the bottom of the second inning. Batting right-handed, he hit the first pitch from lefty Juan Pizarro harder than any ball I have ever seen live before or since.

In 1964 the playing field in Yankee Stadium was truly enormous. The stands at the foul lines were quite short (296 feet down the right-field line and 301 feet down the left-field line), but the fences extended obliquely from there, resulting in a 407-foot right-centerfield and a truly otherworldly left-centerfield of 457 feet. Dead center was 461 feet away. A couple of years later, the Yankees re-marked it at 463 feet.

The ball that I saw Mickey hit in 1964 was a low line drive that barely cleared the shortstop's extended jumping reach. It kept going until it hit the wall at the 457 mark, perhaps 6 feet above the ground. It bounced off the wall directly into the glove of White Sox center fielder Mike Hershberger, who was probably no closer than 40 feet away. Hershberger turned and fired to second, but not in time to get Mantle, who had nothing more than a long double.

Had Mick gotten just a tiny bit of lift on the ball, he would have hit a truly titanic home run, probably farther than 550 feet. I doubt that the ball ever rose above 25 feet on its trip out to left, which projects to a minimum velocity of something around 160 miles per hour.

[Ed. note: After Mantle hit the above rocket off Pizarro, he later scored on an Elston Howard home run, keying an 8-3 Yankees win over the White Sox. It was the first game of a doubleheader; in the nightcap, Mantle was held hitless, though he drew a walk, but the Yankees won, 4-3. Reliever Hal Reniff, who saved the first game, got the win in the second.]

Mantle swung a big bat and flashed a big smile, but it turns out he also had a big heart.

Focus on Sport/Getty Images

A Meeting in Center Field

By Richard Bucci, New York, New York

In a game I attended with my father at Yankee Stadium in 1966, or possibly 1967, a young man in dark clothing and dark hair jumped onto the field and ran toward Mickey Mantle. He caught the umpires and security personnel off-guard and succeeded in getting to Mantle in center field. (That's my recollection—center field—and one reason why I think it must have been 1966, the year before Mickey moved to first base. I would have been 10 or 11 years old, and we were in reserve seating along the left-field line.)

Anyway, Mantle didn't run away from the intruder; rather, he stood there, and the man was able to approach him. The two exchanged a few words and then shook hands. The cops arrived, of course, huffing and puffing, and took the man away, in handcuffs, as I recall. I don't remember if the crowd cheered or booed.

Only the next day did my father and I find out, in a newspaper, the reason for the young man's run. The story, which reported Mantle's own remarks, said the man had been drafted and was likely to be sent to Vietnam. He wanted to talk to Mickey Mantle before he was shipped out, in case the worst happened over there.

At that point, the fighting had become bloody, and I believe this was known even at that time. Tens of thousands of Vietnamese were killed that year. Each month up to that point in 1966, hundreds of U.S. draftees were being killed and about 1,000 were being wounded. My memory is that the poignancy of the man's encounter with Mickey Mantle was not lost on the writer of the newspaper account—or the readers.

That I have remembered the encounter for more than 40 years supports the idea that the man's gesture was understood at the time. He wanted to speak to someone who meant a lot to him, in case he would not return from the war he was forced to fight in. The encounter—and the way Mickey received the man on the field—affected me.

Like every young Yankee fan then, I loved Mickey Mantle. Joe Pepitone might have been my favorite player, but Mickey would be the one to talk to if you were being sent to Vietnam by LBJ to kill or be killed by people you had "no quarrel with," as Muhammad Ali said of his attitude toward the Vietcong.

Mickey Mantle so obviously had a big heart.

WORLD SERIES

Mantle's Yankees won the World Series in 1951, 1952, 1953, 1956, 1958, 1961, and 1962. They lost in 1955, 1957, 1960, 1963, and 1964. Mantle still holds the record for most World Series home runs.

YEAR	AGE	G	AB	R	H	RBI	2B	3B	HR	SB	CS	BB	SO	BA	OBP	SLG	OPS
1951	19	2	5	1	1	0	0	0	0	0	0	2	1	.200	.429	.200	.629
1952	20	7	29	5	10	3	1	1	2	0	0	3	4	.345	.406	.655	1.061
1953	21	6	24	3	5	7	0	0	2	0	1	3	8	.208	.296	.458	.755
1955	23	3	10	1	2	1	0	0	1	0	0	0	2	.200	.200	.500	.700
1956	24	7	24	5	5	4	1	0	3	1	0	6	5	.250	.400	.667	1.067
1957	25	6	19	3	5	2	0	0	1	0	2	3	1	.263	.364	.421	.785
1958	26	7	24	4	6	3	0	1	2	0	0	7	4	.250	.419	.583	1.003
1960	28	7	25	8	10	11	1	0	3	0	1	8	9	.400	.545	.800	1.345
1961	29	2	6	0	1	0	0	0	0	0	0	0	2	.167	.167	.167	.333
1962	30	7	25	2	3	0	1	0	0	2	0	4	5	.120	.241	.160	.401
1963	31	4	15	1	2	1	0	0	1	0	0	1	5	.133	.188	.333	.521
1964	32	7	24	8	8	8	2	0	3	0	0	6	8	.333	.467	.792	1.258
Totals		**65**	**230**	**42**	**59**	**40**	**6**	**2**	**18**	**3**	**4**	**43**	**54**	**.257**	**.374**	**.535**	**.908**

ALL-STAR GAMES

Mantle was selected to the American League All-Star team in 16 of his 18 seasons. Here are his All-Star numbers. (Note: Major League Baseball hosted two All-Star games in the years 1959 through 1962.)

YEAR	AGE	POS	AB	R	H	RBI	2B	3B	HR	SB	CS	BB	SO	BA	OBP	SLG	OPS
1952	20	DNP															
1953	21	CF	2	0	0	0	0	0	0	0	0	1	0	.000	.333	.000	.333
1954	22	CF	5	1	2	0	0	0	0	0	0	0	1	.400	.400	.400	.800
1955	23	CF	6	1	2	3	0	0	1	0	0	0	1	.333	.333	.833	.1.167
1956	24	CF	4	1	1	1	0	0	1	0	0	0	3	.250	.250	1.000	1.250
1957	25	CF	4	1	1	0	0	0	0	0	0	1	1	.250	.400	.250	.650
1958	26	CF	2	0	1	0	0	0	0	0	0	2	0	.500	.750	.500	1.250
1959	27	sub. RF	0	0	0	0	0	0	0	0	0	0	0	.000	.000	.000	.000
1959	27	CF	3	0	1	0	0	0	0	0	1	1	1	.333	.500	.333	.833
1960	28	CF	0	0	0	0	0	0	0	0	0	2	0	.000	1.000	.000	.000
1960	28	CF	4	0	1	0	0	0	0	0	0	0	1	.250	.250	.250	.500
1961	29	CF	3	0	0	0	0	0	0	0	0	0	2	.000	.000	.000	.000
1961	29	CF	3	0	0	0	0	0	0	0	0	1	2	.000	.250	.000	.250
1962	30	RF	1	0	0	0	0	0	0	0	0	1	1	.000	.500	.000	.500
1962	30	DNP															
1963	31	DNP															
1964	32	CF	4	1	1	0	0	0	0	0	0	0	2	.250	.250	.250	.500
1965	33	DNP															
1967	35	PH	1	0	0	0	0	0	0	0	0	0	1	.000	.000	.000	.000
1968	36	PH	1	0	0	0	0	0	0	0	0	0	1	.000	.000	.000	.000
Totals	**52 games**		**43**	**5**	**10**	**4**	**0**	**0**	**2**	**0**	**1**	**9**	**17**	**.233**	**.365**	**.372**	**.737**

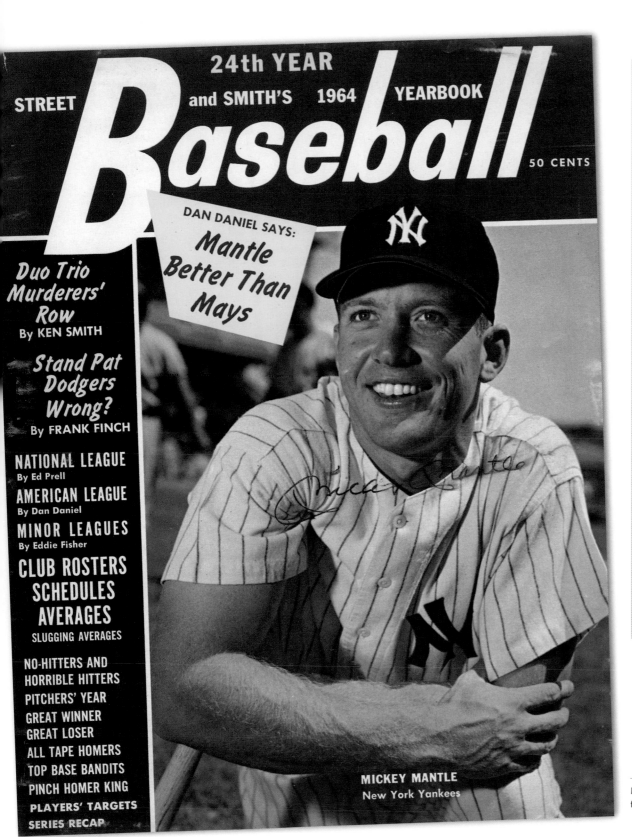

MEMORIES OF MANTLE

By the Numbers

Funny thing: a contemporary baseball fan might look at Mickey Mantle's numbers, scan the statistics, and wonder what all the fuss was about. He had a .298 career batting average—pretty good, not great. He had only four seasons with at least 40 home runs, and only four seasons with at least 100 RBIs. How does that compare with Albert Pujols? Barry Bonds? Alex Rodriguez? Even Rafael Palmeiro?

Needless to say, the stats don't begin to tell the whole story. During the era in which Mantle was playing, there were only a handful of players with comparable statistics. "Substances" weren't a factor (alcohol aside), and, perhaps most important, pitchers were provided with much more room for error than is the case these days.

— Stuart Freeman, Brooklyn, N.Y.

Mantle, the most beloved and feared man in baseball.

Casey Stengel once said that "managing is getting paid for home runs someone else hits." If so, "The Old Perfessor" had plenty of cause to thank Mantle, his star pupil, for his paycheck as skipper of the Yankees.

Robert Lerner/Getty Images